The Edge of Success
An Underrated Legacy

By

Kendall Belvedere Helmly

Dedication

This book is dedicated to my parents, lest I would not be here. I owe everything to their love and kindness.

Contents

Chapter 1:
The Carpenter's Place

When you are the fourth child in a family of six siblings (3 boys and 3 girls), it is hard to get noticed unless one is a prodigy or a criminal. The rest just go unnoticed until the meat tray gets passed to them at the dinner table. I was neither gifted nor ballsy enough to steal anything worthwhile, making me very ordinary, in other words, invisible. When I think about it, the ability to disappear in plain sight could be useful at some level. My place at home with the other children was secure.

My oldest sister, Melissa, almost eight years my senior, dealt with all the teen dating issues. She set the career bar high, graduating from law school and passing the Bar exam on her first try. Roger, my older brother, is an engineer living out of state right now. Beatrice, the middle sister, is a Platoon Sergeant in the U. S. Army. Then there's me, Willie, the carpenter. Oh yes, let us not forget the twins. Carson the artist, and Katherine, the auto mechanic. I was the baby until they showed up, thanks to modern science and a boatload of fertility drugs.

I was young, around four, but I recall vividly the odd collection of noises coming from Phillip and Martha's (Dad and Mom's) room during conception. Most times, it sounded like an African safari documentary. I would just giggle along with my older brothers listening outside the door. I think Dad may have been happiest when Mom finally got pregnant with twins. He got to go to bed early. I wasn't so crazy about my forthcoming siblings.

As if the eight months prior weren't intense enough with all the planning and redecorating, everything had to be perfect for the new arrivals. Twice over! I ended up living in a converted attic. I resented the hell out of being moved up there at first, but around the age of ten, I discovered that my attic was the largest room in the house, according to floor space. Also, because of all the geometry, i.e., the roof pitch, it probably influenced my choosing of carpentry as a profession. I set my bed up so that I could see the night sky lying in bed. The constellations would put me to sleep every night, weather permitting. I would lie in bed at night and gaze up at the stars, wondering to myself, as all young boys do, what my place in the universe really meant. I was a November baby. My zodiac sign was Scorpio. The passioned hopes and dreams my folks had of me becoming an astronomer or physicist were shattered upon entering high school and the advent of teenage girls. After that, I was fixated on the pursuit of more tangible assets.

I enjoyed shop class. I started with lamps and ashtrays, then evolved into dovetail dresser drawers. My shop teacher, Mr. Fields, asked me to build a shed for the Phys Ed dept. After that project, I felt like I had a real future as a carpenter. I got hired as a gopher in the summer of my junior year in high school and have been a carpenter ever since. I was hooked from the first day. My first boss, Mr. Brentler, took me for coffee one rained-out morning and told me, "Son, you will never be part of a profession that is more rewarding than carpentry. When you and your crew complete a new housing project, it means there is one less homeless family in the world. The benefits of home ownership are too numerous to mention. It can be a one-bed, one bath ranch house, all the way to a 25-room mansion. A family will occupy that new home, and another family will have the opportunity to live in their old house. You give a family permanent shelter one project at a time. It's important that you grasp the scope of that responsibility. When it's the end of a really hot day, and you don't think you can lift another piece of sheet rock, remember who the real benefactors of your labor are. Always carry that with you." I have never forgotten those words.

I love my dad dearly. He provided for the entire family extremely well as a CPA and financial planner. Scholarships or family funds paid for my sibling's college tuition. That was a big help. I chose not to go to college - I am the outcast. Even Beatrice plans to go to college after she retires from the service. Katherine went to a well-recommended technical college. She is certified to work on electric, hybrid, gas, and diesel engines. I was so proud of her when she graduated. We were very close growing up, and we looked out for each other. She even beat a guy up for me before I had a chance to tangle with him. That was Katherine, the tomboy, who started turning wrenches in high school. That hot rod of hers is a thing of beauty.

I really considered going into the Navy as a Seabee, but Paul Brentler promoted me to site foreman, and I decided not to enlist. Mom was happy that I didn't choose a career in the military. She almost had kittens when Beatrice signed up. Bea wants to be a medical technician when she gets out of the Army. I am the only one left without plans for higher education. Camden went to art school and now lives in my old room in the attic, which doubles as an art studio. He has a very promising career as a painter, even though technically, he still lives at home with his parents.

My folks always tried to support our career decisions. Of course, they wanted us to strive for the greatest amount of success possible, but they weren't totally crushed that I chose not to go to college after graduating from high school. I think Mom and Dad realized I had real talent as a carpenter. Dad took me fishing one sunny Saturday morning, just the two of us, soon after I received my diploma. I got his blue collar vs. white collar speech. He told me I would have a gap between retiring from pounding nails and eligibility for Social Security. He had seen so many blue-collar clients come in for financial advice, usually fifteen years too late. I know he meant well, but I wasn't listening. I did take his advice on saving money and avoiding vices. In eighteen years as a carpenter, I have over fifty grand squirreled away. I have no plans to buy a house, though. I will probably rent for the rest of my life. The last thing I want to do when I get home from work is stare at some honey-do list. Sorry, Vee (my girlfriend), but when I come home, I just want a burger, beer, and a bed.

Lately, I have been catching lots of flak for not being on board with her about marriage and children. We have been dating for over a year now, and she wants to move in together. I can see where she wants to be in five years. A nice four-bedroom house, two kids, two cars, and a big mortgage. I have concerns about a housing recession looming on the horizon. I'm sure that I am just too close to the industry, and yet, I am not the only one with misgivings about the construction industry. My boss, Paul, is paranoid, too. At the end of the day, I want the same things that Vee (Veronica) wants, sure, but the economy is so cyclical at times. There have been housing bubbles before. I have never experienced a slowdown in my profession, but Paul is confident that one is coming in the fairly near future. He says it is necessary to keep housing prices attainable for the middle class. Honestly, the way housing prices are increasing, the middle class is getting pushed right out of the market. That said, it bears no how I feel about Vee.

I love Vee dearly; she is a delight to be with. I feel so happy when we are together. Honestly, I can't imagine myself not marrying her eventually. I also know that the minute we move in together, she will make me stop using a condom. I think back to what Dad told me a while ago, "Son, if you want to have an extended career as a carpenter, you will need at least half a million dollars in savings before the age of fifty. Then you will be in a good financial position to retire from construction on your own terms and pursue a less physically demanding second career. At that point, you have financial freedom to do basically whatever you want. Go back to school, start a business, sell real estate, etc." Vee wants that now. I don't know how much longer I can keep her at bay.

She will never agree to wait another five or six years to have children, no matter how convincing the argument I present to her. Vee keeps blasting her biological clock in front of me. I can't really blame her. I am really looking forward to the day that we move in together. It would mean getting a larger apartment or a small condominium. Twelve to fifteen hundred dollars a month would be ideal. That would get us a two-bedroom, one bathroom. We could be very cozy there. Again, I know it would not be just the two of us for very long.

The phone rang. It was Vee confirming our dinner date tonight. Dinner in forty-five minutes at Monty's. Every time I go in there with Vee, I get the same look from Monty. "So, when are you going to propose to this gorgeous woman that you love so much?"

I look back and telepathically affirm, "Not tonight. Keep the cork in the champagne bottle." Vee and I arrive in separate cars as usual and meet in the foyer. Monty greets us in his usual subtle way. "Good evening, Mr. and Mrs., oops, spoiler alert, I hope." Then I roll my eyes and retort, "Okay, Monty, can we have our usual table? Thank you."

"So, Vee, how was work at the bank?"

"Not bad, they posted the positions available at the new branch opening across town. Ted Wilmer, our district manager, asked me to apply for the assistant manager position personally. I think he may have me on his short list. The money is better, likely a four to six-dollar-an-hour raise. It is more headaches, though."

"Did you say he requested you to apply?"

"He told me my last evaluation was very impressive, mostly due to the day I engaged the silent alarm and stopped that daylight robbery."

"Oh yes, that was amazing. What tipped you off that something was wrong about that guy?"

"Mostly, it was the insulated jacket he was wearing on a really hot day. Nobody is that cold when it is 86 degrees outside. Also, he was casing the building the moment he walked in the door."

"Good luck, sweetheart, I will be praying for you."

"Will, if I do get the promotion, can we at least consider moving in together?"

"Okay, I will seriously consider it."

"Thank you, baby. Do you want to stay over at my place tonight?"

"Very much, honey, a stampede of braying beasts could not falter my arrival."

At seven am the next morning, I awoke to the smell of bacon, eggs, and freshly brewed coffee waiting for me at the breakfast table. I never met a woman so thoughtful, kind, and selfless in bed or otherwise. We planned to go camping at the beach the following Friday and Saturday night. It's autumn. The nights will be chilly. That means no bugs, not even gnats. Three days of surf fishing at my favorite spot, and two nights of campfires and snuggling in our sleeping bag built for two. Weather permitting, the Atlantic sunrises are breathtaking, especially if you have a companion to share them with. Vee looks stunning as the sun cascades light rays upon her gleaming bodice. I am left speechless, caught in the spectacle of another seafoam dawn.

Chapter 2:
Foundations and Forecasts

Vee's interview went very well. We are just waiting for the month-long background check to go through. I swear it is like the governor himself must grant us a boon. Vee has been more nervous than her two cats, Tiki and Fluffy. Apparently, she has a great-uncle who got arrested for grand theft. I can't believe they would hold that against her. She worked in her family's hardware store before getting her Associate Arts degree. Vee was hired almost immediately as a bank teller.

I was lounging on my couch watching football when Vee burst through my door, pounced on me, showered me with kisses, and yelled, "I got the job, I got the job. When do we move in together?"

"Wait, I said I would seriously think about it." Then she kissed me about a hundred times, ripped off my shirt and pants, then proceeded to seduce and tease me into a frenzy. "Okay, okay, we will get a place for the two of us and the cats." Undenounced to her, I found a place a week ago and put down a deposit for the first of the month. Three bedrooms, two baths, and a sunroom/porch. I think she is going to love it. The only stipulation is that we keep using birth control. Let the nest egg double in size. She agreed.

"Okay, mister, but after that we get engaged." I agreed. It only took us just over two years to squirrel away another seventy-five thousand. All we ever did was make love and go camping, usually at the same time. It is amazing when you find a companion who seems to appreciate everything you do for them, and at the same time forgives your minor miscues, no questions asked. I know at the end of the day, there is someone in my life that I can count on to reinforce my positive energies when I lose focus on what is important. That is a great comfort to me.

Vee and I went to Monty's to celebrate our engagement. Monty was completely beside himself, making sure everything was impeccable for the occasion, the champagne, the balcony table, the violin serenade, and a six-course meal. I told Monty I could get used to this. I don't think I have ever met a more conscientious ambassador for the hospitality industry. Monty is elegance personified. I cherish his friendship dearly.

We set a budget of $10,000 for the wedding. Even Mom and Dad were impressed by how much money Vee and I were able to accumulate in just five years. Vee is thirty-three and I am forty. Vee makes $45,000 a year now. All my salary goes right into savings. If we buy a small house, I could conceivably be a house husband, but I don't think that would be ideal. If Vee were to receive another promotion, that scenario would be feasible, but I don't see Vee being promoted to branch manager any time soon, unless we are willing to relocate elsewhere. I love Savannah way too much to leave. Our families are here. This is where I want to build our future. Vee has strong feelings for this area, like I do. We are driven to succeed, but not at the expense of our happiness together. Patience is a good thing. Love combined with patience can be very rewarding, especially when one is infatuated.

I am a little concerned the housing market may be softening a bit. Dad keeps saying the stock market is strong, but housing, not so much. It could be a housing bubble. I have always trusted my dad in the past, and I have no reason to doubt him now.

I got up early this dry crisp Saturday morning and made French toast, Vee's favorite. We made love well into the early morning, so I let her sleep a little longer. Vee walked into the kitchen, walked up to me, flashed me with her bathrobe, grabbed my ass with both hands, and whispered in my ear, "Good morning lover." Then she gave a smile and sat down at the table. "Oh, you made French toast, my favorite. You must want to go fishing today."

"No, sweetheart, I was just wondering how much you want to buy a house?"

"Willie, you know I want us to buy a house. I realize it will cut our monthly savings in half."

"Not necessarily, if we downsize our pickup trucks to small SUVs, we should be okay. We are both going to need a new vehicle at some point in the next twenty-four months anyway. The real trick when it comes to vehicle ownership, as you well know, is equity. If we combine the trade value of our trucks with a cash sale for two small SUV's we can eliminate a car payment. That is a one thousand dollar a month savings right there."

"You want me to give up my truck for an SUV?"

"Yes, Vee, we need to purchase more family-oriented vehicles. I hate to give up my pickup truck, too, but at some point, it will become necessary. It basically comes down to whether you want yearly vacations or big, oversized vehicles. I vote for yearly vacations. The trucks are paid off, now would be a good time allowing us to maximize our trade-in allowance. Remember I Corinthians, time to put away childish things."

"Did you say family-oriented vehicles?"

"Yeah, I did, honey. I want to marry you. I want to give you my name, my heart, and everything that is physically possible to give. I want you to be the mother of my children."

"Oh, I figured I would get the kids from Charlie. He is here almost every day."

"Charlie the mailman, that's my competition? I thought you always had a thing for Victor, the bartender at Monty's. You stare at his ass enough."

"I stare at your ass too. Honestly, Will, I would have to do both of them together to get over you."

"That's more like it. You are starting to make me jealous. Come over here woman and dig your fingernails into my sweet ass."

"Kiss me, lover."

"Honey, I love you."

An hour later, we came back to the kitchen and reheated the breakfast I had made earlier. There is still the issue of whether to buy a house or keep renting. I think a small 4-bedroom, 2 bath on a one-acre lot is very achievable, if we downsize the vehicles. Even if the economy tanks, we will be okay for a few years as long as we stay healthy. If I were to get injured at work, there would be very little to fall back on. I would have to do like Dad said and find another profession. That would mean going back to school for three years minimum.

My best subjects were math and history. I could teach high school. I could teach wood shop or English. Not English. History, that would be cool. Where to start? I was dual-enrolled during my senior year in high school. I completed four college courses. One trip to the administration office should have me matriculating again. I don't think now is quite the right time.

Paul is about to retire or will in the next year or two. If the owners hire from within, the job is mine. The position pays about 65K a year, plus a company vehicle. I was the interim office manager when Paul had hip surgery. Jack and Wayne said I did a fantastic job, and the bonus I received when Paul returned was very generous. I do worry that the company is growing ahead of the local housing economy. Jack assured me that as long as interest rates stay relatively low, we will be okay. I have always trusted Jack in the past, but this is the first time that he and Dad have conflicting forecasts. Dad does not trust the housing market right now. Also, he's been recommending his clients roll over into low-risk funds for the next nine to twelve months. Dad has our long-term investments ready for a possible volatile turn in the economy. Housing prices are inflated right now. Even though Vee and I could, it doesn't mean we should purchase a home at this time. It is just not a good time to invest.

I feel strongly that Jack and Wayne are ignoring some significant warning signs of a major shift in the housing market. They keep telling me that housing trends tend to be localized, and typically, they are not affected nationally. I have never lost money listening to Dad's advice. My gut tells me, God forbid, Jack and Wayne are headed for a fall.

Chapter 3:
The First Saturday in June

Vee loved the apartment that I found. We were completely moved in by the first of the month. I really liked having a den. I finally had a place where I could go and be undistracted. I have always been fascinated by this country's history. This is my library. It's quiet, cool, and nostalgic. If the need or opportunity were to present itself, I would seriously consider returning to college with the goal of pursuing a bachelor's in history. I would really like that. Maybe get a master's degree and teach. Who knows? Vee is very excited about the sun porch. Tiki and Fluffy have a place to hang out with Vee when she gets home from work. Cats are amazing creatures, complete with their own very original personalities. They both accepted me as one of the family. I usually get up way before Vee does in the morning, and both cats get up and join me when I go in the bathroom to shower and shave. I have to give them some love every morning, or they won't let me leave the bathroom. That's the easy part, because Tiki and Fluffy are very affectionate cats. They are both completely house-trained. As long as they are fed twice a day and the litter box is clean, the cats are very content. Neither of them like going to the Vet, though. Getting them in pet carriers can be a chore. The minute we pull them out of storage, Fluffy and Tiki run right under the bed. Now we put them on the porch with Vee before I retrieve the carriers.

Vee and I finally decided on a venue for the wedding. Forsythe Park in downtown Savannah. We met there a little over six years ago. It was a political rally for the incumbent mayor. Dad dragged me to it with Mom, and I have been thanking him ever since. Dad must network and make appearances. We ran into another of Dad's friends, Hank Sterling, and his daughter Veronica. We all stayed for the fellowship/picnic immediately following the rally. Vee and I started talking and discovered we had several common interests. Mostly, an appreciation for the outdoors. We started dating almost immediately. She was getting ready to graduate from college and already had a job lined up in a local bank. I took Vee to Monty's on our first date. Monty knew at first glance that Vee and I would end up together. Call it hospitality ESP. Whatever the circumstance, Monty was right. Vee stole my heart from the very first kiss. There is a moment that all lovers share when they lean into one another for a sustainable kiss. The expectation of warmth, grace, and tenderness which precedes a sublime moment right at the edge of ecstasy, prior to being bathed in a sea of passion. That terminable kiss is the start of an avalanche of conjugal exploits that will linger and endure in our hearts for many years to pass. So memorable it will clasp our two souls in harmony, forever adhering them in amorous delight. That first kiss, a chance to reveal my soulmate. The warm, wet response as tongues purposefully collide ever so softly. This is the foretelling of kinetic passions that bow before a soul's desire to be loved. As I exited her porch, I did not want to graciously exit her abode for the evening. I wanted desperately to lie with that woman. I was completely infatuated with her.

I hadn't felt this way about anyone since my first girlfriend in the tenth grade. Wendy Ellis was a grade ahead of me. Mentally, she was gifted. She was my first, and much more experienced. I was nervous and needed help with the condom. Wendy gently guided my hands until the condom was securely in place. Then she whispered in my ear, "See, you can do it, you just need a guiding hand."

Wendy was wonderful, and I wholeheartedly understood from that point on that it is much better with a partner to share the experience. We were only together for a little over a month before she graduated early and moved to Massachusetts to start her first semester of college. A couple of phone calls, and it was over. The sex was great, but I was never going to provide the high-powered lifestyle that she was preparing herself for. I was a delicious distraction, prior to starting her life's journey. Right now, she is in med school. She finished law school and passed the BAR last year. I think she wants to work in forensics. I can say I knew her when. I learned a lot from Wendy. She taught me how to be loving and supportive of someone, but still allowing them to grow as a person and not be smothering. The last time we were together, Wendy and I talked for quite a while afterward. She broke the news to me that she was going off to college early.

We also talked about how important it is to allow your partner to grow as an individual in the relationship. It's okay at first to be together constantly, but once the infatuation starts to wear off a little, you will find out how much they mean to you. You should discover their wants, needs, goals, and desires. If they're similar, then you have someone to grow and flourish with. If not, you need to move on.

She told me, "Will, you are always going to hold a special place in my heart. You are kind and so polite. I wish that my goals and dreams were yours as well, but I think we both know you are rock solid with your family ties here in Savannah, and I am a butterfly in the crosswind. I will miss you dearly as a friend and a very gracious lover. I have no doubt you will make someone a fantastic husband someday. Promise me you will not grow up too fast. We never saw or spoke to each other again, except for her phone calls from school. I didn't enjoy those phone calls very much. It really hurt that I was never going to see her again. I think it is true that one never completely gets over their first love. It took a few years to get over Wendy, but if I hadn't endured that relationship, I would not appreciate Vee as much as I do. Veronica is the woman that I want to spend the rest of my life with. Right now, at this very minute, I am committed to making Vee happy for the rest of her life. I found out at the picnic in Forsythe Park that she was someone special.

Vee was very pretty, but it was her kind and generous character that really appealed to me. Vee's parents, Hank and Cindy, were wonderful. Hank started out as a carpenter like me, and now he owns a commercial development firm, in addition to being friends with half of Savannah. He is not a politician, but I suspect he has quite a bit of influence in town. Vee makes my life seem so simple when I am with her. She loves camping at the beach. I could cuddle up with her in front of a campfire for hours. I know our hearts are content.

It is Monday morning. I am up at 6:00 am, getting ready for work. She slips in the shower with me, and we get all lathered up together. We rinse off and make breakfast together. As we are sitting at the table together, Vee asks, "Will, did you speak with the Parks and Rec. office yesterday?"

"Yes, I did. The first week of June is wide open. I was a little surprised that no one had booked that weekend yet."

"Okay, let's book the first Saturday in June. I can hardly believe it is less than 4 months away."

"Me neither. Hey, I am not betrothed to a fiancée with cold feet, am I?"

"No lover, my feet are toasty warm. Seriously, how do you feel about a wedding planner? Dad is planning to invite a lot of his friends, approximately two hundred or so. With the rest of our family and friends, we will be looking at over five hundred people attending the reception. I think we definitely need to hire a wedding planner. Even with that extra expense, we should still be under budget. Plus, all mine, and your dad's fat cat friends will load up my bridal purse very well. At my sister Missy's wedding, they averaged two to three hundred dollars each. She told me they paid my dad back for the wedding and bought her a new car with the leftover cash."

"Okay, honey, I'm all in for that, it will mean less running around for us in the end, right?"

"For sure, sweetie, then I will make a call tomorrow."

Four months flew by very quickly. I turned down the bachelor's party in Atlanta. That's for the guys who haven't seen enough naked women prior to getting hitched. I can certainly do without the giant lap dance cum stain on my trousers. I think Wendy and the few others that I slept with prior to meeting Veronica put those misogynistic notions far behind me. After Wendy, none of those women could even come close to Vee.

I do wonder sometimes what kind of dad I will be. This world, as it exists now, moves so fast that it seems reckless at times. How will Vee and I be able to keep our children out of harm's way? How did Dad and Mom manage to raise six kids and have every one of them turn out successful? That is quite an accomplishment for any generation to pull off. I guess it boils down to love, patience, and kindness. Love, that is the tricky one; many times, Mom and Dad had to be the bad guys with us kids to make sure we had our priorities straight. Like when I told Dad I wanted to start a marijuana farm out west. Actually, it was a hemp farm, but why split hairs? Dad talked me out of that, but it wasn't easy. His hair was a little grayer after that conversation. Or when Beatrice wanted to go on the road as a bass player in a punk rock band. The six of us definitely threw Mom and Dad a few curveballs growing up. No matter what crazy idea one of us got stuck in our head, they listened. When Beatrice told them she wanted to join the Army, I think they were actually relieved. She has done so well in the Army.

The first Saturday in June is here. My tux is all laid out. Little brother is my best man. He stayed over at our place in case just to make sure I wasn't the one who got cold feet or decided to go on an all-night drinking binge. Truth be known, Carson was the one who polished off all the beer left in the fridge. I have to give him credit for following his dreams. His paintings are inspiring. He is definitely a modern artist with a retro flair. Carson is going to Paris this upcoming fall to apprentice for approximately one year. The man is so excited. He is also no starving artist. Three of his works sold at auction recently for over forty thousand dollars. That is no small piece of change. The folks were so happy for him. He has another show coming up next month. I expect him to do very well.

***

Three hours left before the big ceremony. I guess it is time to start getting dressed. I can't wait to see Vee in her wedding dress. I will try not to cry when I see her walk down the aisle. I would speculate that it is a very surreal moment standing at the crossroads of bachelorhood and betrothal. Coming to the realization that the single man that I once was will be no more. Much of the high-spirited camaraderie I shared with friends and cohorts will probably disappear. I am not the reckless soul that I was five years ago. I still go camping, but now, when I wake up bundled in my sleeping bag, my soulmate will be beside me. I will get to gaze into her lovely hazel eyes, study the politeness in her smile. I will lean over and kiss the corner of her mouth and watch her wake up and embrace me. Holding her snugly in my arms, I would ponder how many other newlywed husbands attain the same semi-erotic glimpse of true happiness.

Carson bangs on my bedroom door and yells, "Get up, you lazy oaf, or you will be late!" I hopped out of bed, scratched my nuts, gave a big yawn, stretched, and walked into the bathroom as I peered into the mirror right in front of me. I was instantly aware of every flaw, blemish, and wrinkle attached to my body. Why is Vee marrying this out to pasture post-thirties? Because I love that woman and she loves me, that's why. I proceeded to shave twice on purpose. I don't want any five o'clock shadow, even though we are getting married at 2:00 pm.

Chapter 4:
Wedding Vows and Warning Signs

Partly cloudy, eighty-one degrees, with a slight breeze, was the radio announcer's weather forecast as I listened en route to Forsythe Park. I could not ask for a better day in June. I was a little concerned about it being too hot, even under the pavilion. Surprisingly, I was very comfortable in my penguin suit. The gallery was full. The DJ played the wedding march, and Veronica walked so elegantly down the aisle, escorted by her dad. I was ready to bust something; she was so beautiful in that dress. One thing is for sure: I definitely married up. Vee was stunning, a vision. I thought to myself, I get to hang out in public with this woman. Wow, I better behave myself, no scratching, picking my nose, or my seat with her around. Actually, Vee and I are past the no flatulence stage in our relationship. Now we just leave the bathroom door open when one of us is on the throne. That's everlasting love in its purest form. We lived together for a good amount of time before this day. American society puts so much emphasis on sexual compatibility, I really wonder what it would be like if the bride and groom were both virgins to sex. They might need an interpreter, and maybe the mother-in-law could come along. No, no, no. Bad idea. Just purchase a sex manual. I think that would be a more practical solution. Or one of a million sex self-help videos. I cherish every opportunity I have to be with Vee. We are overwhelmingly compatible. All I have to do is see Veronica come into the bedroom wearing a sheer lingerie ensemble, and I am all done. Every time we engage each other in a romantic embrace, I learn something new about Vee; even if it is just an extended kiss, the effect is the same. My heart is content with the knowledge that I am loved.

Judge Andrews asked me, "Do you, William, take this woman to be your lawful wedded wife?"

I said, "I do, I do." I don't know why I said it twice, but it sure felt good repeating my answer. Veronica responded the same. Then we leaned in and kissed each other. I leaned back and gazed into her eyes, and kissed her again. This one continued much longer than the first. We stopped when the gallery started whistling and cat-calling. Then it was a short walk to the limo and off to the reception. We ended up inviting over five hundred people, and I think they all brought a friend. There was a boatload of guests in that room. The wedding planner, Mr. Cashman, requested four bar stations, four buffet lines, and table service. I thought it was a bit of overkill, but he was right on the money, no pun intended. The rotisserie chicken was delicious. Veronica's dad paid for all the food and alcohol (open bar). Vee and I managed to greet every table. Everyone seemed to have a glorious time. We cleared over

$25,000 after expenses. Not a bad day financially. Off to the honeymoon.

Yellowstone was always gorgeous this time of year. The snowcaps, the wildlife, the natural wonders, the trout fishing, it was spectacular. Our honeymoon suite in the main lodge was breathtaking. We did lots of picnicking around the park. I liked getting up early to go fishing in Lake Yellowstone. The water was crystal clear. We were kind of undecided whether to honeymoon in Hawaii or Wyoming, but the first morning we woke up and walked out on the elevated patio connected to our room, we knew we had made the right decision. The view of the lake and snow-covered peaks in the distance was something neither one of us will forget. Plus, the price was half of the Hawaii package. We will probably go to Hawaii on our twenty-fifth anniversary. The ten days we were there went by way too fast. I guess the mark of a grand vacation is the fact that it is always too short.

We arrived in Atlanta late and decided to stay overnight and drive down I-16 the next day. Sort of a vacation from the vacation. Wyoming was so big, open, and free. I would love to live out there, but I would starve as a carpenter. Vee and I have started to build a nice life for each other in Georgia, and I want to raise my family here.

I returned to work after my two-week furlough. That old tool belt was a little heavy the first day back, but I soon regained my stamina. I had the misfortune of coming back to the jobsite during drywall day. Luckily, Vee gave me a few full-body massages with those wonderful healing hands of hers. It's worth all the difficult work just to get the awesome rubdown from Vee. It usually culminates in a happy ending for both of us. Then we snuggle up on the sofa with the cats and watch a little TV.

There have been rumblings around the office concerning an overabundance of housing in our area. No matter what the planners and engineers tell Jack and Wayne, they are still convinced that our firm is recession-proof.

Jack keeps telling everyone, "Look, even though housing prices are high right now, there is still a demand for new housing in the Savannah area. People are still moving here." Dad sees the same thing and warns everyone of a huge bubble in the housing market. I think Dad is right. I don't know how or when something is going to happen, but I can feel something bad looming in the not-too-distant future. I have convinced Vee that now is not the time to trap ourselves in a big mortgage. Neither of our jobs is recession-proof. We are vulnerable. We need to minimize our expenditures and max out our savings for twenty-four-months at least.

I didn't think much of it three months ago when I overheard a conversation between Wayne and Jack, I probably should not have. I came back to the office to retrieve a set of blueprints, and I stopped off and used the bathroom. As I sat there on the porcelain throne, I was privy to an interesting conversation. Wayne was on the phone with Jack and said, "Jack, make sure the realtor knows we are only interested in conventional loan applications or cash offers for the Colorado acreage. Emphasize cash as the first choice. We want to close quickly. Thanks. See you back here tomorrow."

I never really gave it another thought until a few weeks later, when I glanced over at Jack's desk while waiting for some Certificate of Occupancy paperwork. There were two creditor delinquent notices on top of his desk. In the fourteen years I have been employed with the "Davis Group Developers," that is the first time I have ever seen them utilize unsecured debt. Jack and Wayne swore up and down that they ran a cash business. No house was ever built without securing a buyer. I think I need to have a conversation with Paul. It could be nothing, but the way housing appraisals are going higher and higher, I think Dad is right about a national housing bubble on Wall Street.

If this is true, it could be 1929 all over again. No, I am just paranoid. Moderate fluctuations in housing prices have always been specific to one or two areas of the country. People speculate that it is too hot in Florida or too cold in New England, and move elsewhere. We have the NCUA and FDIC to protect us. Well, at least our cash is safe. Not like in '29 when everything crashed. Just for peace of mind, I am going to call Paul this afternoon.

"Hello, Will."

"Hi Paul, can we meet for lunch or coffee somewhere today? I would like to talk to you about something, but not over the phone."

"Sure, how about at "Big Earl's Coffee" in an hour?"

"Perfect, see you then." I packed up my tools for the day and called the office and request some personal time for the rest of the afternoon. Then I headed out to meet Paul at the Café. I arrived first and ordered a dark roast with extra cream. The barista brought my order over. Paul walked up right behind him and ordered an Americano coffee, medium sweet.

"Okay, kid, what is up?"

"Paul, I have been getting some very strange indications at work. Is the company okay financially? The reason I ask is that Wayne and Jack have been extremely curt in telling me that everything is fine. Also, I heard Wayne talking about selling their Colorado spread. That has been in their family for over

100 years. It sounds like they are pooling their assets to ride out a fluctuation in the housing market. Am I wrong?"

"Well, yes. You are right. Jack told me one of our major investors filed for bankruptcy about two months ago. They have not been able to secure another buyer for the project, and it is not just us. New construction has slowed significantly all over the South. Even out in the west, prices are down. Everyone is nervous. You told me that Phillip suspected a housing bubble in the market. It looks like he is right. At this point, it may be just a matter of time before Wall Street shows signs of a bear market. I will tell you this. The last major subdivision that we built, only 78 of the 110 units sold at full price. The rest went at a reduced rate, some over 20% below the original list price. You know as well as I do that the six previous projects sold out a year before completion. We have never had any issues finding buyers. The market is starting to dry up."

"Do you have any idea why this is happening? What is causing the housing bubble?"

"Okay, I probably should not be passing this information to you, but since you asked, I was bar hopping last week, along the riverfront. I ended up next to a banker who was really tying one on. He started talking about all the refinancing that was going on right now. He also said that most of the people receiving loans now would not have been approved five years ago. He called them band-aid loans. People come in with no equity in their home, getting approved anyway. What this guy was telling me was scary. The worst part was that he and Vee worked for the same bank."

"No way, the same branch or the same company?"

"Relax, kid. I don't think it was the same branch; he was some bigshot loan officer in another office. Still, our conversation sobered me up fast. I don't know how much of his banter was the booze talking or him, because he was slamming them back pretty good. Personally, I rolled all my investments into extreme low-risk funds, and I recommend you and Vee do the same."

"Too late for that, Dad already moved our entire portfolio into low-risk funds."

"Paul, you just turned sixty-six, right?"

"Yes, I could retire tomorrow if I wanted to. My plan is to wait for the market to adjust and reinvest, or I could hedge, but that takes more expendable income than I have available right now. I do worry about our company. I have seen this industry at what I would consider its lowest point. That is when carpenters are working as dishwashers and flipping burgers at the Drive-Thru's. This can be a very cruel business at times. You, my friend, have done very well for yourself. A beautiful wife, money in the bank, and the opportunity to create a real success for yourself. So, Will, what are your goals for the future?"

"You know I love building things. These last 16 years have been very rewarding. It is like you said, providing permanent shelter for people is a blessing for me and the new homeowner. I think that may be why Jesus was a carpenter. But the reality may be just what you said. If the housing industry is in jeopardy, then I have to be prepared to weather the upcoming storm. As you pointed out, I am well-healed financially to ride out a six-month-to-one-year layoff from work. I think back to something that Dad told me. He said that working as a carpenter would force me to retire several years before I could start drawing social security. I considered going back to college and becoming a teacher. I think I would really enjoy teaching high school social studies. I could also sell real estate. I could sell real estate while waiting for the industry to bounce back. I am concerned about Vee, though. You said that *drunk* worked for the same bank that she does. What if both of us lose our jobs? Vee wants to start a family soon."

"Look, you can't worry about everything all at once. For what it's worth, I think you would make an outstanding teacher. I see you work with the young guys and girls on your crew, and you are a born leader on the jobsite. You have patience, knowledge, wisdom, and experience; your subordinates like working for you. In the last 12 years, you have been a site foreman, and I have had way fewer issues with your crews than others. You create value in their work ethic. I know you are going to great things no matter the profession."

"Thank you for the kind endorsement. I realize I can only be President of these United States for eight years. Do you have a preference for a cabinet post on my staff?"

"Okay, smart guy, seriously, I think you would make a great teacher."

"Thank you, Paul, I really appreciate that. Lately, I have been reading quite a bit about our history. I find U. S. history very interesting, especially the colonial era. Once I got past all the romanticism attached to the expansion west, I started to see how raw and uncivilized many parts of it were. Specifically, the way Native and African Americans were degraded as second-class citizens. If I were to return to school, that would be my focus. So, it would seem from our conversation that you foresee a volatile future for the entire U. S. housing industry like I do."

"Yes, I don't know when, but I think the how may already be in motion. Think about it for a moment. What would happen to housing prices if all these so-called band-aid loans started to go under? The housing market would be flooded with foreclosures. Wall Street would not be immune to this major hit either. I would think this would not be good for banks. What does Phillip say about this?"

"I am going to talk about this with Dad today. I was planning to crash his office today and pick his brain. I feel he is going to repeat parts or most of what we discussed as inevitable, given the lack of oversight in the housing industry right now."

"Can I go with you? I would like to hear what he has to say firsthand."

"Paul, how did you and Dad meet?"

"Oh boy, you know that your dad and I were classmates in high school." I nodded. "Well, we were both smitten with your mom. She was quite beautiful back then, and she has taken really good care of herself, in fact, your dad as well. The three of us were chummy back then. I eventually realized that I had no chance with your mom. Your folks were meant for each other. A year later, I met Gertrude, she was my true love until Multiple Sclerosis got her. I can't believe it has been six years since her passing. Your dad and I were pretty tight back then. Phillip and I used to go hunting and fishing together before you were born. Your old man was a crack shot with a rifle and one of the best game trackers around. I still hang out with Phil from time to time. He is easily my oldest and dearest friend."

"I thought you met in college. I didn't realize you went to high school together. Just between you and me, what was Mom like in high school? Was she a player?"

"She was wild back then, the Disco Queen. Your dad, too. They were regulars at the local discotheques."

"Come on, not Mom and Dad. But they are so kind and reserved, I can't imagine them boogieing all night long."

"Will, I got news for you, kiddo, everybody is young once, even me. Not to change the subject, but we need to get going here soon."

"Okay, I will meet you at Dad's office in an hour. I have to go home and take a shower after hearing about mom and dad; I feel very creepy and dirty right now."

"See you in an hour."

Chapter 5:
Storm Warnings and New Beginnings

I had to make a couple of stops along the way. My old framing hammer was starting to show its age, so I decided to treat myself to a new one. I stopped by the hardware store and bumped into Vee. She was visiting with her cousin Mark, who now owns Ridi's Hardware. Vee's aunt Mae and uncle Ridi started the store decades ago. It is amazing how much of a following that store has. People love coming because of Mark's huge inventory and superior product knowledge. I told Vee what I was up to with Paul, and she wanted to join me as well. Apparently, work is all abuzz over the spike in home prices. The trend is that, due to overcrowding and staggering prices, people are relocating south, where houses are much less expensive. I think if this trend continues, what I consider the southern middle class will start to disappear. This may create a wealth gap among native retirees. People may have to sacrifice many of the small luxuries they have become used to. Hopefully this turns out to be nothing, but I am still going to tread very lightly with my expendable income in the immediate future. i.e., find hobbies that make money, woodworking, leatherwork, and arts and crafts. There is no sense in planning a trip to Europe and having to worry about money the entire time. I don't want to agonize over every appetizer and espresso. Vee and I will be okay for a while, we're still in the lustful newlywed phase. Sometimes I love that woman so much it hurts.

Paul had already arrived at Dad's office when we pulled up. Vee and I scurried inside to greet Dad. The four of us walked into the conference room, and Dad quipped, "To what do I owe all this attention? Everybody is okay, right?"

"Yes, Dad, Paul and I had an interesting conversation about recent indicators in the Housing Industry, and we wanted to get your feedback. Then I bumped into Vee at the hardware store, and she came along." Dad got up immediately and closed the door.

"Okay, let's talk about this, but not here. Sometimes the walls have ears. I will call Mom and tell her we are coming over for lunch. Does BBQ sound good for everybody?" We nodded. "Perfect, I will get takeout on the way to the house. I will meet you there in 45 minutes."

We all got in our vehicles and headed for Mom and Dad's place. I wasn't quite sure what was going on. Dad usually kept things close to the vest, but I never knew him to be so cautious conversing at work. Dad must know something, but what? It can't be good if he does not want to repeat it in his office. Maybe Wall Street is not as concrete an investment as the so-called experts say. I was the first to arrive, so I went in and gave Mom a big hug. Carson came down the stairs from the attic.

He took my old room when I moved out. He also has a small studio up there.

Mom said, "Dad will be here in a few minutes, come on and help me set the table. I want to hear what Phil has to say, too. If I know your father, it will be good for us and bad for lots of people who are not as prepared as we are. That includes Melissa and Roger, also. I love those two, but they are stubborn as mules when it comes to taking Phil's advice about anything. After all, he is a CPA. I just hope if and when the chips fall, they don't end up on their heads."

I retorted, "What's going on?"

"Wait for Dad, he will explain everything." I sat down at the dining room table and poured myself a glass of ice water. Paul and Vee walked through the front door and joined me at the table. They inquired why Dad is being so secretive. I repeated what Mom told me: just wait for Dad.

I did inquire about mom's disco days. Mom went upstairs and retrieved a photo album. Apparently, Mom and Dad won a local dance contest in 1977. They looked amazing in their dance costumes. Mom asked, "How did you find out? As if I can't guess, Phil told you, didn't he? Darn you, you never could keep a secret."

"Sorry, Marty, oh oops, Martha. Oh crap."

My siblings and I shouted, "Marty!"

Mom quipped, "Paul, that's it, you are officially off my Christmas card list. I suppose you told them I dated you before Phil."

"No, you just did." Then everybody broke out in laughter. Dad walked into the room with both arms full of delicious-smelling BBQ. We all proceeded to dig in for the next ten minutes. Then I asked Dad what was going on. Why did he insist on continuing our conversation here at home instead of the office?

"Okay, people, hang on to your bloomers, there is a huge bubble in housing prices, like three hundred percent or higher in some regions of the country. When banks and other lenders start seeing a high number of foreclosures and bankruptcies it could cripple Wall Street. This will eventually impact world markets as well, but not nearly as severe as the U.S. economy. My colleagues and I are very concerned. Now there is an upside. We, I mean people who know it is coming, will reap by reinvesting after the crash. I see all of our portfolios growing by over two hundred percent. Just be patient, there may be bank closures. I don't think there will be any bank runs like in 1929 due to the FDIC, but it could get messy. I recommended that my clients spread their liquid assets among several banks for the time being. The FDIC only insures up to $250,000. Don't keep all your eggs in one basket. Well, folks, that's it. There is a financial storm out there. Whatever rumors you heard about a bubble are true. Will and Paul, your bosses, could be hit really hard if they are not ready for this. I hope that everyone at this table knows that I will be willing to do whatever I can to help you through this if push comes to shove. FYI, I am part of a growing minority having big concerns about where Wall Street is right now, I wouldn't be too vocal on this topic right now. Many of my peers are not willing to admit what may be coming. I hope I'm wrong, but all the indicators are there, I'm not wrong! Not about this."

I asked, "How long before we know for sure?"

"A year, maybe less than that."

"More ribs, anyone? Come on, don't let it spoil your appetite. Lighten up, people, it's not WWIII, just a housing bubble." Everyone went back to chowing down on lunch. Dad always had a way of de-escalating a tense mood. Vee and I headed back home after the impromptu lunch discussion with everyone.

Truthfully, I am not sure how to feel knowing that something this jeopardizing is looming on the horizon. I am glad I have Vee to go home to right now. The weather outside is overcast and balmy, with a hard chill in the air. I am feeling a little depressed. I arrived back home first. I went in and headed for the fridge to grab a beer, then walked out onto the patio and sat back into the lounge chair and let myself escape for a time. Tiki found my lap, and the two of us shared company for a while. I don't know how she does it, but Tiki cat has the uncanny ability to know when I am feeling poorly about things. I have pretty much convinced myself to at least explore the possibility of pursuing a degree in History. I do wonder what Vee will think of the idea. It does mean we will be down to one income while I matriculate.

"What do you think, Tiki? Can I handle college at my age? I haven't done anything in the way of school in over ten years. I don't even know what classes to sign up for."

"Meow, meow, puurrr."

"Okay, if you feel that strongly about it, then I definitely should at least sign up for a few classes and finish my Associate Arts degree."

"Meow." Tiki jumped off my lap and made a beeline for the garage. I heard Vee's truck pulling into the garage. She walked in and found her way to my lap. She kissed me multiple times, then proceeded to hold me and lie on my shoulder. "Will, I love you more than the stars could ever allow a woman to be in love. Make love to me."

I stood up and scooped Vee in my arms, carried her to the master bedroom. I laid her gently on the bed and placed myself beside her. We began undressing each other, touching one another, caressing, kissing, fondling, and stroking all over and over again. We were, at that point, committed to the confluence of shared passion. I dared not speak for fear of losing any slight portion of the ecstasy we shared at this very moment. She brought me to the honed edge of complete sexual awareness, and I was immensely grateful. We lay in each other's arms for several moments prior to my falling into a deep sleep.

I woke up to the sound of our stereo. Vee has quite an extensive record collection from the '60s and '70s. It's hard not to be nostalgic about that musical genre. I walked into the kitchen, and Vee was making glazed salmon with all the trimmings. Perfect timing, I was famished. She plated and served everything while I sat down.

"Vee, I am considering going back to school and finishing my Associate's. Do you think now is a good time for me to approach a career change?

"Yes, honey, I do. We are more than capable of paying for it, even full-time. I strongly recommend you go full-time. I started working part-time in my first year, still helping in the hardware store. One day, soon after completing my first semester, Uncle Ridi sat me down in his office and basically told me I was fired. Well, not in the usual sense. He was telling me to go to college full-time. My folks could afford to send me to any college I wanted and pay for everything, no questions asked. Back then, I felt some obligatory sense to pay my way through school. Uncle Ridi was able to do what Mom and Dad couldn't: convince me to devote all my energies toward my education. So, I started full-time the next semester. I won't say working your way through school isn't a good way to sharpen your time management skills, but you have no issues in that department, my love. Balancing work and school at the same time is a pain in the ass, especially during finals. Go talk to an admissions counselor and enroll for January. You are going to do fantastic. You are still leaning toward History, right?" I nodded. "Good, you already took trigonometry while dual enrolled. Your math is done. concentrate on English. History majors write a boatload of articles and essays. Do you know what you want to do afterward?"

"I am not quite sure at this point. I could teach high school, get my bachelor's, and go to law school, or paralegal. I'm sure something will materialize sooner or later. I will make an appointment tomorrow and talk to the administration."

Minutes after I got off the phone with administration, I started to get a case of cold feet toward the whole idea. I kept asking myself why I deserve this opportunity to change careers. It is getting tougher to run up and down extension ladders on cold, crisp mornings like this one. I won't miss that at all.

Chapter 6:
Trading Tools for Textbooks

January is two months away, so I don't have to turn in my resignation for several weeks. I do want to give Jack and Wayne plenty of notice. They have been so good to me. I am looking at this not as an end, but a new beginning to a grand adventure. Something down deep inside my gut is telling me I must do this. I am about to reeducate myself. Hopefully, I will become a better man for Vee, my love.

The following Monday morning, I marched right into Wayne's office and handed him my resignation. He was completely blindsided by that. I explained that my long-term goals did not involve the construction industry. Wayne could see that I was passionate about my decision and respected me enough to accept my leaving the firm without a fight. Then he sat down and wrote me a severance check for five thousand dollars and graciously thanked me for sixteen years of loyal service. The office staff threw me a wonderful going-away party, complete with a big cake and lots of presents. Jack and Wayne tried to convince me to pursue a degree in construction engineering. They both said I would breeze through it. I had considered going that route at my first notion of returning to college, but at this point, I see myself moving in a different direction. While I was building houses, it wasn't hard to bring a strong work ethic to the jobsite every day, but internally, it wasn't what I was passionate about. Those sixteen years were very instrumental in forging my character and willingness to give something of myself in every project. It was always vital, weather permitting, to finish the job on time. Other individuals and their families depended on me to provide them with a safe and secure place to live while raising a family. I will venture forward from my first career with an immense sense of closure.

My first day back in college saw me sitting at a desk waiting for my economics professor to walk in. I was so nervous, but all my anxiety was for naught. After the first lecture, I fell right into the curriculum. It took about a week before I really started to feel welcome in my new surroundings. My first study group cemented that idiom for me. I liked my history classes the best. Being a bit older than most of my classmates, I became the old sage in both of my study groups. Vee was spot on when she said I would be writing a ton of articles and essays. I struggled a bit at first, but very soon, finding ways to build a successful argument got easier. I started developing a strong passion for U. S. History.

It became very apparent early on that attaining my associate degree in history would not quell my thirst for learning at this point. I wanted my bachelor's and possibly a master's in history. I became fixated on that end. Upon completion of my Associate's, I quickly transferred to the University of Savannah to finish my four-year degree. University life was a little bigger, faster, and definitely more challenging. No more 500–1000-word essays. Most were 2000 minimum. At least two per subject.

As I sat securely back in my den, surrounded by history books, I gazed out my window at a society in crisis. Dad's forecast of a severe adjustment to every market index on Wall Street came in a little over eighteen months. Vee and I only took a three percent hit to our retirement portfolio, thanks to Dad's insight. Melissa and Roger did not fare nearly as well. They both lost over half of their savings in one week. Roger's engineering firm had to downsize by seventy-five percent to keep their doors open. Roger, along with hundreds of other engineers, planners, and builders, was laid off with no timeline for being rehired.

Melissa fared much better. Her law firm started focusing on bankruptcies and foreclosures, which seemed never-ending at first. Roger is now living back at home in his old room with Mom and Dad. That turned out to be worthwhile because a month after the housing crash, Dad suffered a mild stroke. It was a wake-up call for all of us kids. Mom has started to slow down a bit as well. Roger has been able to help with the more physical tasks around the house. I have been taking care of all the maintenance issues, which, as the house starts to show its age, are many right now. Most are just cosmetics, but I have had to do some upgrades. Walk-in showers for all the bathrooms, ADA doors, etc. The day that Roger arrived back home, I was out front by the garage when he pulled up in some little Italian two-seat sports car.

Roger hopped out and said, "What do you think of her?" I thought it was cute, at least it had a hard top. "Will, you should get one of these for yourself. I think Vee would love it." I told him, "No brother, I am not interested in revealing the size of my penis to everyone I pass on the road. I will spend my money on stocks and old furniture, thank you, sir. Why don't you sell this thing and bankroll yourself for several years?"

"No way, I love this little thing."

"Suit yourself, Roger, old boy."

After Roger found himself unemployed for over eight months, he finally came to his senses and sold the little green snot rocket. I think he finally got tired of me teasing him about it. Nevertheless, he downsized his vehicle and pocketed almost seventy thousand dollars in the process. I know it must have been very difficult for him. Roger frequently talked about weekend road trips through the Blue Ridge Parkway. I can see how that would be a wonderful way to spend a weekend with a companion. Unfortunately, Megan, his significant other, prior to being laid off, left him shortly after he was officially let go. I liked Megan. She was a nurse practitioner. But she wanted desperately to marry a rich man. You can't blame a young woman wanting to marry a man with means.

Security and future sustainable assets are very desirable qualities in a soulmate. With some bird species, the female looks for the male with the nicest nest. Why should Megan be any different? Roger wasn't rich quite yet, but he had much potential to retire as a full partner with all the trimmings. Sad thing for Roger, he is at that unfortunate age between very hirable and early retirement. Forty-seven to fifty-five is a very difficult time to try and start over with a new firm unless one has upper management experience. The poor guy is facing some hardcore ageism. He may have to consider obtaining a teaching credential to close the gap before retiring. He could maybe do a startup. He may be living back home with Mom and Dad permanently. I guess there are worse things in life. It might turn out that after two decades, the only thing Roger will have to offer is a small 401 (k) and a new car that is paid for.

The only real difference between Roger and me, besides the age thing, is a sizable portfolio. Mine scales his by 400%. Plus, I am having a pretty good time reinventing myself in college. I just wish there were more opportunities for a history major. I had a notion of being a paralegal. I would get to do research. That is something I find very intriguing. Private investigators also interest me, but I would want to work for a legal firm, not on my own. I still have another three semesters before graduation. I could be a librarian, no, definitely not a librarian.

I just saw my career counselor, Barbara Sims, yesterday afternoon. She told me that one key element to getting hired quickly after graduation was to complete as many internships as possible. A high GPA translates to being task-focused, but internships get you hired and promoted over your peers. I thought that was very good advice, if I could only figure out what I wanted to do. I have always enjoyed building things, and I like old stuff. Barbara said, "If that is the case, then archivist may be a good fit for you. Would you like me to inquire about internships or externships near us?"

"Yes, that would be wonderful, thank you. I would be very interested."

"Will, I have a former roommate from college who works in the campus Natural History Museum. I will reach out to her and pass along your information."

"Again, Barbara, thank you." I headed for the campus library to finish a medieval studies paper. I was very excited about the opportunity to work in a museum setting. I speculated on possibly working on a historic display. That would be very cool. I was always very impressed with the amount of detail involved.

Less than a week later, I got a voicemail from Barbara Sims. She wanted to talk to me right away. I stopped by her office the same day.

"Will, come on in and take a seat. I spoke to my old roommate, Shawn Britton, and she wants to set up an interview with you. She was very interested in your carpentry background. Apparently, they have been without a carpenter/builder since the beginning of the semester. Call her ASAP."

"Yes, I will right away, thank you so much. Have a very blessed day." I left her office and called Shawn immediately.

"Archives, hello."

"Could I please speak to Ms. Britton please?"

"This is Shawn. How can I help you?"

"My name is Will Burrows."

"Will, the carpenter. Can you come over right now?"

"Yes."

"Okay, when you get here, go to the ticket counter and ask for me."

"Sure, I should be there in about fifteen minutes." The second I walked through the door, Shawn met me immediately and took me back to the carpentry shop. Wow, the room was a disaster. 2 x 4 board ends all over the floor. Yards of sawdust were scattered everywhere, and hand tools were slung from one end of the room to the other.

"What the hell happened here?" I said.

"Our last carpenter moved away on us, and we have been on our own for over a month. I spoke with your old boss, Paul. He said you are the best. Can you start today?"

"Yes, I am, and I can. It will take me a couple of hours to put this room back in working order."

"Will, do you want some help with that?"

"No, just keep everyone out of this room and change the locks. You and I will have the only key to the millwork shop. I insist we keep it that way. You are lucky nobody got seriously injured here. OSHA would have kittens if they ever saw this room. Okay, Shawn, you just hired yourself a carpenter."

"Good, I will leave you to it."

It took over 90 minutes to clean up all the remnants and sawdust. The shop was equipped with a dust collection system. Obviously, nobody was aware of that fact. After a significant amount of elbow grease, the room looked immaculate, and there were only three tools missing. I locked the door and went to look for my new boss, Shawn. I found her in her office, banging away on the phone. Then I asked her what she wanted me to do next.

"Will, we are way behind on our exhibits. I have a stack of work orders you can start with. We have a new exhibition in just three weeks. I have blueprint plans here. How long would it take you to frame this out?"

"With two good men, less than a week. And I don't mean the boneheads that dismantled my millwork shop. Yes, this may be your museum, but that is my millwork shop. I expect every individual who works in it to keep it immaculate." I didn't like pressing Shawn like that, but I wanted her to understand how important accountability was to a man in my position. Honestly, I think she was grateful to have someone take that off her plate. I saw her walk by the shop window later, and I thought her jaw was going to hit the floor. She told me it was the best she had seen that room look in the eight years since they hired her.

I did get some good help. Greg and Brad were both young and competent. We had the first display framed, drywalled, and painted in two days. I hate using the quick-dry compound, but we had no choice in order to make the deadline. I told Shawn I wasn't interested in working full-time due to my course load for the semester.

I told her that I could supervise all the millwork projects, working 20 to 25 hours a week, if I had two more carpenters. With a crew of four, we should be able to cover every deadline. Shawn agreed. I like this part-time supervisory gig. It works well for me. I was almost floored at the wage they offered me. It was very generous on their part, but you get what you pay for, and I am more than competent when it comes to this type of work. I had to consider that at the time, I must have been a godsend to them. Shawn was under enormous pressure to complete several projects that were already on the books.

Chapter 7:
Mourning and Meaning

Surprisingly, working at the museum has not affected my performance in the classroom. I was a bit concerned, but luckily, I am very good at prioritizing my time. So far, I have been able to juggle everything, so much for an internship. I don't think that word came up during my brief hiring process. That reminds me, I need to call Paul and thank him for his outstanding recommendation.

I walked in the front door, greeted by a very vocal Tiki cat. I said, "What's wrong, girl?" Tiki took off for the patio where Fluffy lay motionless. I reached down and felt Fluffy. His body was cold and lifeless. I sat down and picked up Tiki and held her in my lap, patting her head and shoulders ever so gently. I told Tiki that Fluffy was gone now. He has left us, and his spirit is now residing with all the other cats who have passed on from this world. Then I thought, oh shit, I must call Vee and tell her what happened. I picked up my phone and dialed her number.

Luckily, she answered. "Hello, sweetheart, what's up?"

"Honey, Fluffy has passed away." I could hear her sobbing and crying. "I found him on the porch where he expired. Tiki is okay. She is upset, though, and knows that there is something wrong with Fluffy. Vee, are you okay to drive?"

"Yes," she said, sniffling and sobbing still, "I should be okay to drive home. I am leaving right now."

"Be safe, I will see you in a few minutes." I walked to the linen closet and removed one of our nicest couch comforters, then wrapped Fluffy in it. I went outside and cut off a few fresh flowers and put them on top of Fluffy. Then I started to cry. I never realized how much Fluffy meant to me. Every morning, he and Tiki would escort me into the bathroom and stand guard while I took a shower and dragged a razor across my face. Now the task will belong solely to Tiki.

Vee walked through the front door. I immediately hugged her. She dried her tears on my shoulder as I escorted Vee to the patio where Fluffy was lying, adorned with flowers.

"Vee, sweetheart, would you like a drink? A whiskey perhaps?"

"Oh, yes, that would be nice, thank you." I dashed off to the liquor cabinet and made us a pair of wet giraffes. That's what I call a whiskey highball on the rocks. When I returned to the patio, Vee had stopped crying.

"Will, do you know how it happened?"

"No, I came home, and Tiki was meowing loud and ran right up to Fluffy. He had already passed when I got here. He was seventeen, right?"

"Yes, I told myself this would eventually happen, but one is never ready to let go of a part of the family, pets, or otherwise."

"Vee, sweetheart, I had a coworker lose his dog about five years ago. He called a pet funeral service. Ron, that's his name, said the service was very respectful and not all that expensive. I think he said his pet was cremated. That would be a nice tribute; don't you think?"

"Will, did I tell you how much I love you today?"

"No, I don't think so, but I can see it in your smile, feel it in your caress, kiss."

"My sweet man, hold me tightly, make me know that I am loved."

"I am here for you, baby, whatever you need." We just stood there for several moments in one another's arms. We sat back down and finished our drinks. I looked up the pet funeral parlor and called. I spoke to a very polite gentleman who agreed to come over and take possession of our little loved one. Mr. Castille arrived approximately an hour later and told us it would take approximately three to four days to perform the cremation. All that he required of us was to come by his office, select the urn, and escort it home the same day. This made Vee very happy. All the arrangements were wonderful. There was a small chapel where we sat and said our final goodbyes to Fluffy, then escorted his ashes back home for safekeeping.

I don't think I ever really considered how devastating losing a pet can be. My siblings and I grew up without owning a pet, so I never had to deal with that type of loss. Neither Mom nor Dad grew up on a farm, so they had no experience in that department. Plus, it meant another mouth to feed. Now, every time I look at Tiki, I have to catch myself from dwelling on the fact that Fluffy is not with us anymore. They were two peas in a pod. I am surprised by how Tiki is taking the fact that Fluffy is no longer with us. She seems to be content now being the lone cat in the house. Tiki must have found peace with the loss of her companion in her own way. I guess, like everything else, it is time to move on.

Fluffy's death made something very apparent to me. Later generations seem to have fewer coping skills when it comes to consequences. I was shocked by how much the death of a pet affected me. The experience left me emotionally vulnerable until I allowed myself to grieve properly with respect to Fluffy's passing. Vee was devastated for several days. Eventually, we were able to find closure, but it was somber around the apartment for a few days. Tiki was a big help to Vee in her semi-depressed state. The passing of Fluffy aside, it just seems that young people are so stressed out.

Even something as simple as an error ringing up an order in a drive-thru restaurant caused a stressful chain reaction. I placed an order, and the cashier mistakenly charged me for the bill belonging to the vehicle ahead of me in line. When the manager came over, they tried persuading me to pay the other patron's bill. I mentioned that their bill was considerably higher and expressed my concern regarding its fairness. The manager had a hissy fit right in front of me. At this point, I just wanted to forget the entire incident. I guess my point is that the cashier and the manager did not consider the fallout from their mistake. I didn't think that it was a big deal to refund me the difference between the two bills. I was wrong.

I have been noticing a pattern in young people and a lack of ability to solve problems as they arise. I remember what Paul told me when I started working for him about the humanistic value attached to building new homes. I tried to pass that sentiment onto new crew members, and for the most part, they were receptive to it. For many of those youngsters, it seemed like it was their first conversation concerning personal sacrifice for the well-being of others; it was certainly a teaching moment. Maybe that is why I had thoughts of working as an academic.

Mom and Dad kept the six of us very well grounded when it came to taking responsibility for our mistakes. It's fundamental to the maturing process that every person goes through during their lives. I have doubts whether young couples my age are preparing their children to cope with the consequences of their mistakes. With that in mind, I am concerned that this lack of mentoring could lead to a weakened sense of morality or less emphasis on legalism. I am noticing that younger generations have sensitivity issues. What could happen during a nationwide crisis, like what is unfolding in the housing industry? What will become of a shrinking middle class and an expanding lower middle class? If I had to guess, I would speculate that there would be a sharp rise in homelessness throughout the country due to the lack of means to secure adequate housing. Then there are the mental health issues, which could lead to a rise in suicide. I guess we will all see what unfolds.

Chapter 8:
Blanks and Blessings

Graduation day for me is finally here. I am officially a college graduate with a bachelor's in history. I did it. Now what? I guess I will accept the offer from Shawn, promoting me to full-time at the Museum. My official title is Operations Manager. I would oversee Receiving, Shipping, and Millwork/Construction. Again, this would take much more off Shawn's plate and free her up to put more emphasis on fundraising. I think I am going to like continuing to work here. Mom and Dad were so proud when I walked across the stage and received my diploma. I was damn pleased with myself too. Some of those midterms and finals were tough to get through. It's not easy cranking out fifteen hundred words in an hour. I had to know my stuff. Talk about stress and consequences, that was it.

Don't get me wrong, I love what I do at the Museum. The work that I do daily impacts so many lives in a positive way. Everything, from being a positive influence for my subordinates, to being part of the creative process, and building new exhibits for our patrons to enjoy. But I do miss the hands-on stuff. Working in the Millwork shop. Framing, texturing, and painting the displays. I miss that single moment when a project is complete, and I look back and tell myself my skill, my sweat, made something worthwhile. Now I get the opportunity to manage the expertise of others in a tandem creating process. Now, that is rewarding enough for me. Besides, I don't miss the swollen joints and sore back. Much anguish for a moment's gratitude. I will console myself by living vicariously through my younger, more physically fit employees.

Honestly, I get enough hands-on stuff just keeping up with the old house. Dad is really starting to slow down, and Mom is not far behind him. It seems like every week, something is leaking, peeling, or cracking somewhere in the old place. I would like to hire a full crew to do an entire remodel inside and out, but now, due to fiscal complications, there are more people residing there. Carson could probably get a place of his own, but Roger is stuck there for the immediate future until he can build up a decent portfolio again. Beatrice is retiring from the military in eighteen months and plans to live at home while going back to school. Prior to that happening, the entire interior will need a fresh coat of paint and a new roof. I am not equipped to complete either of these projects by myself. Fortunately, I have already upgraded the plumbing and electrical to meet the existing building codes, and the bathrooms are all ADA compliant. The big issue is the kitchen. The cabinets are shot, but Mom won't budge on having them replaced. I can't really blame her. She prepared thousands of delicious meals in that kitchen. I know I was there for most of them. I guess a coat of paint and a few new hinges will have to do.

Saturday afternoon found Vee and me lounging on the beach yards from our favorite campsite. It is about seventy degrees and breezy. Perfect for a weekend at Savannah Beach. The fish weren't biting much, though. I only managed two decent-sized whiting and a barely legal Redfish the whole trip. I was ok with the slow fishing action; Vee kept me very busy with other actions. She mostly wants us to get pregnant. I agree it is time. We have the means to start a family. Oddly enough, we have been literally banging away with no positive result. I realize we have only been trying for a couple of months, but Vee has never been on the Pill. I figured the first time I didn't use a condom, she would very soon be with child. Nothing has happened so far. I am going to get checked out by a doctor next week, when I get back to Savannah. Vee got a clean bill of health several months ago from her gynecologist, so we are fairly sure it isn't her. I need to know. We need to know.

Sterile, the doc told me 100% sterile. I have been shooting blanks all my life and did not know it. I told the doc I racked my nuts pretty hard on a 2 x 4 a couple of times. He told me that it is probably not the reason. After examining me, he detected no physical abnormalities. I just happen to be one of those lucky or unlucky men, depending on your perspective, who are infertile. I walked out of the office, got in my truck, and sat in my truck alone, weeping into my steering wheel for a while. My elbow slipped down and engaged the horn button. It started blaring. I immediately sat back up as the startling noise broke me out of my depressive state. I wiped the tears from my face and thought to myself, I really wanted to be a daddy, it's not fair, God. I started weeping on the steering wheel again. Why don't I get to have a kid? I'm a good man. I'm a real good man. I love my wife and family. I go to work every day. I don't even cheat on my taxes. This sucks! I dried my eyes on my sleeve and proceeded to drive home. I walked in the door and made a beeline for the booze and poured myself a wet giraffe neat. Screw the ice. I sat in the dark for a long time, waiting for Vee to come home from work, wondering what the hell I did to inherit this. Shit, there ain't no reason for it, I am just an unlucky SOB. Move on, Willie, my friend, just keep moving on. Maybe Vee and I would have ended up raising some criminal mastermind bent on destroying the internet. I don't know. All I do know is how much I hate the fact that I won't be able to have any children with Vee. I guess there is always adoption.

Vee walked through the door and saw me sitting in the shadowy dark, twirling my whiskey glass on the table.

"What's wrong, Will?

"I'm 100% sterile. I'm loaded up with blanks."

"Shit, that's awful."

"That's what I said! Honey, I don't want to adopt a child. God made me sterile for a reason. Let's just leave it at that for the time being."

"Okay. Sure, we can do that. Hopefully, God has other plans for us."

"I am so sorry. I know how much you wanted to make a baby with me. I guess it just wasn't meant to be." I headed for the bedroom, got undressed, and lay down for a long nap. I awoke to a small pair of eyes staring right through me. Tiki came in to say hi to me. I forgot to greet her when I walked in. She curled up beside me. I think Tiki could tell I was hurting inside. About a minute later, Vee walked in wearing a smile and nothing else. Then she slid into bed and curled up next to me and whispered, "I love you very much." I knew then that I was going to be ok from now on and proceeded to fall back asleep. I woke up a little over an hour later to the smell of spaghetti cooking in the kitchen. I hoped she was doing the meatballs. I love that woman's meatballs. She makes them out of summer sausage. They are the best.

"Will, oh good, you are awake. I was just about to come and get you. Can you grab a bottle of Merlot from the wine rack? Thanks. This is ready, let's eat." I uncorked the bottle and sat down, and gazed at spaghetti and meatballs with a tossed salad and dinner rolls. Yum!

"Thank you for cooking this, it looks scrumptious. I am feeling much better now. The shock has subsided a bit. I am disappointed, but I'm okay with it. We have each other to love and cherish. I am very happy to be your husband. Thank you for loving me so much."

"Will you shut up and eat already? The food is going to get cold. You can remind me about all that stuff when we are in bed." Vee always has a way of keeping me grounded, and I love her for it. We finished dinner, filled up the dishwasher, and put in a romcom DVD. Then we proceeded to start making out halfway through the movie. Vee has very arousing appetites.

This infertility thing I am having to deal with is going to haunt me for some time. I feel like half a man. I don't know why I feel so strongly about the ability to sire offspring. I think it may stem from the fact that Mom and Dad did such a miraculous job raising the six of us. For my part, they did a wonderful job raising six kids. Not a bad apple in the bunch, as it were. They instilled in us patience, empathy, confidence, leadership, accountability, and, of course, love. I was so looking forward to passing that legacy forward to another generation of Burrows. It appears that it may not happen. I need to talk to someone before I start to fester inside. I will investigate it on Monday at work. Maybe I can do something during my lunch hour. I like this salaried position thing. I get lots of perks.

Monday, I called the medical hotline at work and was able to make an appointment for a week from Tuesday. I was lucky there was a cancellation. That is how I was able to get an appointment so quickly. Normally, the wait is over a month for an initial consultation. I hope something positive comes from this. I know it isn't my fault, but I feel I have let Vee down by not giving her something she wants, motherhood. Vee would be an incredible mom. I wish I could commit to the adoption process. Hopefully, soon I will be on board with that. Right now, I am still too pissed off with God to consider anything to do with parenting. Even making love to Vee is a struggle. It is a constant reminder of my infertility.

"Like I told you, Dr. Reece, I feel like half a man right now."

"Will, you must understand that this is a major blow to your ego. The ability to procreate is one of the most basic of human traits. At some point in our lives, we all get the urge to have children. Some are stronger than others. From what you have conveyed to me so far, you and Veronica have spent the last several years building up to this moment. To be brutally honest, you have a very tough road ahead. The fact that you are here means that you must care for Vee, as you call her, very much. This is a huge first step. Will, you have many special gifts, don't let this one disappointment keep you from enjoying your incredible relationship with your wife. Tell me, how is your attitude at work? Are you still able to stay task-focused?"

"Yes, no distractions there, it is just at home that I dwell on my infertility. It's as if things were going too perfect, and God, or the Devil, has intervened to throw me into self-doubt."

"Will, I must ask this question. Have you had any thoughts of harming yourself?"

"Yes, doc, usually after I make love to Vee, and during masturbation. I cry after I touch myself. Vee doesn't know. I did it a couple of times, thinking I could rid myself of the bad sperm and be done with it. Then I feel embarrassed and ashamed on multiple levels. I think I literally got that out of my system now. I still anguish over being sterile, but I am smart enough to know that self-gratification is not going to cure me of infertility."

"Good, I am glad to hear you say that, because masturbation will not cure your problem. It could make things worse. It sounds a bit corny, but try and concentrate on the good things in your life right now. A positive mental attitude can go a long way to solidify the healing process in your mind. I don't usually give out my cell number to clients, but you can call me day or night. Please try not to dwell in dark places. It sounds like you have a great family support group to lean on. Don't be afraid to use that. We are almost out of time. I can put you on my schedule every two weeks. Does that work for you?"

"Yes, I would like that, and I will try and be positive and joyous when I am with Vee. I will see you in two weeks." I headed back to work feeling indifferent to our conversation. Keep a positive attitude, sure. That is easy to throw out and see if it sticks. Personally, I am not feeling very sticky right now. I guess I must give it a little time. That reminds me, I have a meeting with Shawn about the new whale exhibit for next month.

I sat down in the conference room, waiting for Shawn and the rest of the exhibit team to assemble. My mind kept wandering back to my therapy session. The rest of the team came marching into the room one by one. Shawn opened the meeting.

"Will, is the frame going to be ready Thursday like we discussed?"

"Yes, the new light fixtures should be arriving this afternoon and installed by Wednesday by the close of business. Then we just need to mount the displays."

"Excellent! Now to new business..." Sometimes I think this job is too much of a comfort zone for me. Then again, if I weren't such a stickler about time management, this place would fall back into chaos like the first day I arrived. This job is not the challenge that I expected it to be, but with all the distractions I am dealing with at home, it is a good thing not to have so many things to stress over at work.

It's four o'clock pm and I have a 5:30 tee time with Paul. I headed out the door and drove to the Country Club for a quick bite before we teed off. Paul walked in and sat down beside me.

"Hello Will, care for a beer before we start?"

"Sure, how is retirement? Are you bored to death?"

"No way. I have dropped eight strokes off my handicap. It's down to fourteen. I am going to catch up to you yet. Now you only have to spot me five strokes."

"Okay, let's see what you have in store for me today. How often are you getting out on the course now?"

"I joined two leagues, and it has made a world of difference. I have finally cleaned up my slice. Sometimes I get lost during the round. I am not used to being in the fairway off the tee, and I don't recognize my surroundings, thank goodness for the course map on the back of the scorecard."

"Okay, funny man, how about you put your money where your mouth is, take the honor for the first hole." Paul addressed his ball and proceeded to smash a frozen rope 290 yards straight down the fairway. If he keeps this up, I will be hard pressed to overtake him. Luckily, he can't putt worth a damn. We are both laying two on the green, and he birdies out on me from thirty feet. That shook me up a bit. The only birdies Paul usually sees are in a pet shop. I managed to make my eighteen-footer and hold pace with him. So much for not putting worth a damn. I won the round by seven strokes, but man, was I impressed with how much he improved his game. He must be playing with the club pro. I shot my usual handicap (81). Paul came in at (88).

"Nice round, forget the five strokes, today dinner is on me. You did great out there."

"I have a confession; I have been pairing up with the club pro for the last two months."

"I knew it. You dirty little sneak. Anyway, that is the best I have ever seen you play. Keep it up, and we will end up sharing the same handicap very soon." I needed a day on the links. It was a welcome escape. Now I just have to get a grip on my infertility when I am with Vee.

Chapter 9:
After the Storm

I pulled into the driveway of our apartment and sat in the car for a moment. This has been a roller coaster of a day, but so far it is ending on a positive note. I walked in the door, and there was Tiki, meowing as usual, wondering where her dinner was.

"Okay, Tiki, I will get your dinner in a minute. Let me get settled in for a bit." Just as I started to open the cat food for Tiki, I heard Vee walk in. She dropped her bags on the couch and gave me a big hug.

"Hi honey, how did your first therapy session go today? Or do you not want to talk about it?"

"It went very well. Dr. Reece told me to concentrate on all the positive things in my life, like our relationship. I am starting to get used to the fact that I can't be a biological father. The only good theory that my doctor could come up with was chromosomal abnormality, but there is really no way of knowing without an autopsy. It's tough to have that procedure while still alive. I really don't want to know that bad. Right now, it can remain a mystery to me."

"Will, honey, would you ever consider an alternative means of me getting pregnant?"

"I don't know, but right now it is just too soon for me to consider it. I'm sorry. I know how much you want to have a child."

"Yes, I do very much want to be a mommy. I can wait a bit. I have time." I could see it was obvious that Vee was dissatisfied with my attitude toward an unconventional pregnancy. I hope it doesn't manifest into a serious issue between us. I don't want Vee to think less of me for feeling this way, but the thought of us using donor sperm to have a child just isn't an option for me. It would be awesome if we could alter Roger's sperm to reflect my DNA, but the technology just isn't there yet. Adoption would be a last resort for me, but Vee is not interested. She believes there are too many unknowns, which is ironic, because I feel the same way about a sperm bank. All I can do at this point is keep praying about it.

My phone started ringing and buzzing in my pocket. Roger was calling to tell me the kitchen sink is leaking. I headed over to Mom and Dad's to see what the problem was. I walked through the back door and saw Mom sitting at the kitchen table crying. I asked her what the matter was, and she told me Roger and Dad were yelling at one another again.

"Why did they do that, Mom?"

"Roger tried to fix the leak under the sink and dad went ballistic again, spouting off about how engineers can't turn a wrench to save their own ass. Roger told dad to eat a bag of shit, and all hell broke loose. I hate it when they get into it. It is becoming more frequent. I think it is due to Dad showing more signs of dementia. He has become much more forgetful lately. When Roger points it out to him, Dad gets very frustrated. Dad is eighty-three, and I am eighty-one. I don't see either one of us responding well to the aging supplements our doctor recommended. Dad is just tired." She began to weep in my arms, "Of living, everything."

I kissed Mom on the cheek and looked under the sink. The problem wasn't the drain, but the hot water valve. I pulled the cold valve too. Both were corroded and needed to be replaced. I ran down to the hardware store and bought a new faucet. The old one wasn't worth fixing. Ninety minutes later, it was as good as new. I reminded Mom that the kitchen desperately needs to be renovated. It's getting much harder to find replacement hardware for the cabinets.

"Son, this kitchen and I have been around for several generations now, and our time is growing short. At this point, I just want us to go out together. You can understand that, can't you?"

"Sure, Mom, I will wait an entire week after you're gone before I tear it down to the studs."

"You little brat! I ought to light up your backside for that." Then we laughed for quite a spell.

"Okay, the kitchen stays as is, but I'm going to buy extra hinges just in case. Honestly, except for the antiquated hardware, it looks very good. Dad kept this house up extremely well. It was built in 1879, right?"

"Yes, but it was not moved to this location until 1959."

"Right, I forgot about that. They don't make them like this anymore. Replacing all the old plaster with drywall made a big difference. It does need a new roof, though. Roger and I will get up there and replace it this weekend, okay? I'm kidding, Mom. I will call a roofing buddy of mine and get an estimate."

Three weeks later, the house had a brand-new roof, gutters, and downspouts. The old place would have fetched quite a price prior to the housing fallout two years ago. Now it is appraised correctly at just over $100 a square foot.

Last time I saw Paul, he told me Jack and Wayne have taken a short hiatus. They plan to resume normal operations sometime around the first of the year. I am worried about Roger. He hasn't mentioned taking any interviews for several weeks. He just scrolls through his phone looking for job leads and hangs out on the couch in front of the TV. I think he is starting to lose perspective. Roger has too much potential to give up on himself at this point. He has to fight harder. Roger came barreling down the stairs. He told us that he apologized to Dad for yelling like he did. That solves nothing. Because after the fight is over, you're right back where you started.

I asked Roger, "Any job leads?"

"I talked to a local commercial construction firm looking for a planner. They wanted to set up an interview, but the salary range was a joke. I told them I would think about it. I thought about it. I will call them. Hopefully, they haven't filled the position. It's an entry-level position. The top pay is 32K a year. There are good bennies, though. I should be able to talk my way into it. Sucks! Before I was fired, I made 85K plus stock options. Now I have no house, no boat, no stocks, no girlfriend."

"Okay, big brother, let's talk about what you do have. Opportunity! "

"Good point, little brother. I do have a shot. At least I'm not working at a sports arena selling hot dogs and peanuts. That is something."

"Your damn right it is. Roger, can I ask you a question?"

"Sure, go ahead, ask me anything."

"What went on between you and Dad that you had to apologize about?"

"Will, Dad is starting to lose patience with everyone in the house. I think he may be starting to show signs of dementia. It is probably a complication from his recent stroke. I am so grateful that you take such an interest in keeping up with all the maintenance issues in this house. I can design it, but I can't maintain it."

"It's okay, keeping this place up to snuff is no bother for me. How would you like to help me repaint the interior? If everyone pitches in, we can get it done in one weekend. I will do the big rooms, if you, Carson, Mom, Dad, and Vee do the bedrooms. Then we can do the hallway together."

"It sounds so easy when you say it like that."

"It's not rocket science. That is your department. Mostly, it is about being well organized and having the right tools for the job. That is where I come in. I will see if I can get a couple of my construction buddies to throw in with us for a steak dinner afterward. Who knows, it may only take one day. Most of them would build a mansion for free beer and a big juicy porterhouse steak. When we are done painting, all that will be left to do is start up the grill and put the beer on ice."

"You can count on me, little brother." The following Monday, I called several of my former coworkers to try and recruit a volunteer paint crew. To my surprise, I lined up twelve people to help me. They all told me it would be a pleasure to help. That meant the family could concentrate on feeding everyone. I purchased the paint and materials, and my recruits did the rest in one day. The house looked fantastic, and there was not a drop of paint anywhere it wasn't supposed to be. Paul even dropped by to make sure the beer was cold and the steaks were cooked properly. He had T-shirts made up for everyone. They read, "Burrows Paint Crew" on the front and "STAFF" on the back. I thought it was a nice touch. I can't remember ever having so much fun painting a house. It was great seeing many of my old colleagues again. It looks like Roger got a couple of solid employment leads. One was even for a management position. Who knew so much would come from a backyard picnic? As I sat down at the table and started digging into my delicious steak, Vee sat down next to me. She leaned over and whispered in my ear.

"Will, you brought so much joy to everyone here today, because of your kindness and generosity. You have many things to be grateful for, and many friends to share in your gratitude."

"Honey, eat your steak before it gets cold," she said, laughingly. "You have been sitting on that line for a while, sir."

Vee was right, everyone had an amazing time at the picnic, which went on well into the night. If it hadn't been so cold, people would have started to jump in the pool. I told Dad to get a heater for it, but he never did. After the beer ran out and everyone said their goodbyes, I had a chance to really reflect upon what exactly took place. Happiness was discovered here today. I experienced happiness for the first time since learning about my infertility. I really got a dose of what is important in life.

I think it might be time to discuss looking into adoption. I would hope that Vee and I would be considered good candidates for adoption. Driving home from the picnic, I asked Vee, "Would you consider adopting a child, or children?"

"Of course, if that is the way you want to pursue raising a child. Sure. I think we have a lot to offer as foster parents."

"No, Walter, whom you just met, was a foster parent with his wife. He told me many horror stories. He said it can be a very bumpy road with all the regulations. Also, the social workers can be very aggressive at times. I would prefer to adopt over foster a child."

"Okay, sweetheart, let's go talk to an adoption agency."

Chapter 10:
The Cost of Love

Dottie Henderson is our point of contact as we educate ourselves in the complicated process of adopting a child through an adoption agency.

"Good morning, Mr. and Mrs. Burrows. My name is Dottie Henderson. Call me Dottie. Please have a seat and make yourselves comfortable. I am sure you have many questions concerning the adoption process. I am here to answer all your questions. First, I do have a few things I would like to know about yourselves. Most of all, I would like to know why you are considering adopting a child?"

"Well, Dottie, Vee, and I cannot conceive a child through intercourse, because I am sterile. This has been verified by my doctor. We are not interested in vitro fertilization, but we are very interested in starting a family. Vee and I believe we have much to offer a child. We have financial stability, a beautiful home, and much love to share."

"Vee is short for Veronica, is that correct? Do you feel as strongly as Will on this matter?

"Yes, very much so. My husband, Will, and I feel this is our best option."

"Okay, I see you filled out the questionnaire. You both are over twenty-five years old and U.S. citizens. We do require a national criminal background check along with submitting your fingerprints as part of the process. Once that is complete, we will come to your house and perform an independent home study. This will be conducted by a social worker.

The entire adoption process, depending on availability, can take up to two years from the date you are approved as prospective parents. Our agency fees are usually between $40,000 and $45,000 per child. This is the point where I ask you if you would like a beverage and leave the room so you can discuss this with each other. Would either of you like something to drink? Water perhaps?" We nodded, "Two waters coming right up."

"45K per kid. What do you think?"

"Will, if we adopted two kids, it would take all their college money just for the privilege. We have got to think carefully about this."

"I agree. I expected it to be less than half of that. We need to crunch some numbers before committing to any of this." Dottie walked back into the room with our bottled waters.

"Do you have any questions that you would like to ask me?"

"Dottie, we were a little surprised at the overall cost. Will and I are going to need some time to think this over and revisit our monetary situation before committing to such a significant financial commitment. I am sorry to have to dilute our decision for adoption down to money, but we want to be sure our commitment to the well-being of the child includes the possibility of post-secondary education."

"Folks, I completely understand. It would appear from your combined annual income that you have that covered. Personally, I commend you for taking that into consideration."

"Thank you, Dottie, but we still need to give this more thought."

"It was a sincere pleasure meeting you both. Here is my card. If you have any questions at all or just want to talk, please don't hesitate to call." Vee and I drove home feeling like we just got whacked in the stomach with a crowbar. Wow, 45 grand just to get the kid, another 20 grand a year to raise them. Then another 50 grand or more for college. How did Dad do it? We all went to in-state institutions and lived at home, that's how.

"Vee, what do you think? I see it as a classic tradeoff. Spend the money for a kid and make them pay their own way through college."

"Will, doesn't Savannah U. have a deal where your children get a reduced price on tuition?"

"Yes, dear, but we can't bank on that. What if the kid excels in a field that isn't offered there? Then we are back to square one. Anyway, I need a drink and some naked time with my woman."

"Oh really, and just what woman is that?

"The mailman's wife, of course."

"You're such a tease. When we get back to the house, I will make us a couple of rusty nails, okay?"

"That sounds awesome. I want to hop in the shower quick when we get home." We walked through the door, I fed Tiki, and Vee made the drinks. We bottomed those up and headed for the shower. It felt good to be distracted from thoughts of adoption for a brief period. Just the two of us, making the most of what we have. Not everyone gets to exploit all their dreams. We still have many gifts to share with one another. I absolutely adore our life together. If that is all God blesses us with, then so be it. That will have to do. I wake up every morning next to a person who shares my love, my hopes, and my dreams. I am blessed. I am so lucky to be able to just sit back in bed like I am doing right now, and glance over at my beautiful wife sleeping after we made love.

Tomorrow is Valentine's Day. I'd better get busy with the card and chocolate candy thing. I can't do flowers. Tiki loves to disintegrate all the flower petals. I made that mistake last year. The cats had flower petals scattered all over the house. I don't know if it is the smell, the texture, or both, but if I send flowers, I have to send them to her office.

Vee loves her job, but being promoted to Branch Manager would require her to go back to school and obtain a bachelor's degree in business or finance. I told Vee she could take a two-year sabbatical and go back to school full-time like I did, but she doesn't seem very motivated to do that. I am concerned she is holding back with the thought of becoming a stay-at-home mom. We need to get on the same page with this family planning of ours. I hope I am not being unreasonable about the whole artificial insemination thing. Using a sperm bank just seems unnatural. Also, going through a fertility clinic, there is a greater chance of multiple births, two, three, or more, during pregnancy. That is not an outcome I would easily welcome. Vee is still asleep. We can talk about that a little later. I'm hungry. A grilled cheese and bacon sandwich sounds good right now. Throw in a beer, tater tots, and a baseball game, and that should round out the evening very nicely. I was just finishing my sandwich when Vee walked down the hall topless and asked me, "Will, where did you go?"

"Sorry, sweetheart, I got hungry."

"Come back to bed and I will let you do that naughty thing you like to do." Oh boy! I clicked off the TV. So what if the game was tied in the bottom of the eighth inning? I couldn't get in bed fast enough. Like I said, I am truly blessed. I think Vee was just warming me up for Feb. 14th. We have reservations for a B n' B in Daytona Beach. We have both been looking forward to this trip ever since we booked it. I say Daytona, it's actually in Ormond Beach, just slightly north. Less traffic, and it's easier to get a dinner reservation. I have to admit there is only one Daytona Boardwalk. The food, the bars, the arcades, and the beach. For us, it still has a very romantic appeal. Just don't go there on Bike Week, unless you really like to party. The only thing worse is Spring Break, absolute chaos!

The next morning, we left very early, dropped off Tiki at the Kennel, and shot straight down I-95. We had lunch in St. Augustine. That is another of our weekend getaway sites. I am like a kid in a candy store. All that history just oozing out of every street corner. Then we drove down A1A to our B n' B right on the beach. Three days of sand, surf, and some of the best seafood restaurants around. We even like to sneak in a little miniature golf.

The first night, we ended up at an excellent Mexican restaurant. I think Vee just wanted a margarita. I asked her why she didn't consider going back to college to secure a promotion at work.

"Will, I can't really see the point. It is not easy to break into the old boy network that still exists in the banking industry. Also, after the housing crash, things are tight promotion-wise anyway. I figure, why rock the boat right now? Maybe later I could address that idea. Now is not the right time. Honestly, we live comfortably on your salary alone. Most of my pay goes right into savings. That is actually a very good point. I really got a dose of sticker shock in Dottie's office the other day, but she is right, we could afford to adopt a kid or two, for that matter."

"Yes, we could, but it would diminish our quality of life. No more trucks, semi-annual vacations, gourmet dining, etc."

"That, as you so eloquently stated, is the tradeoff. I thought you wanted kids, at least two anyway."

"Yes, sweetheart, I do. I just don't want to pay for them. Can we rent them on weekends? Or better yet, rent them out on weekends. Let our folks have them three days a week, like a timeshare."

Laughing, "They would never go for it. We might get them to play along for a year or so. After that, forget it. Well, my only real concern is college. Two kids, average grades, out-of-state tuition, two decades from now, would run us 100K apiece. Oh yes, and we can't forget extracurricular activities. I. E. art lessons, music lessons, sports clubs, travel teams, it adds up quickly. Dad seemed to do it so well, but he was in the right industry. Dad always had at least 50 grand in the checking and savings accounts. Plus, he walked around with several hundred dollars in his pocket."

"My dad did the same thing. But that was back when a single income was enough to secure a household. Now, unless you do what they do, you are living in a dual-income household like us. It's a different time, and certainly a different economy. Shit on us, for not doing what they did."

"Shit on me for having the hands of a carpenter."

"Oh, no way, your hands have many talents besides carpentry. You can bank on that."

"Thanks for the words of encouragement." The server brought our dinner to the table. The food was authentic and delicious. We ordered Flan for dessert. It was scrumptious. After dinner, we headed over to the boardwalk for a nice walk along the beach. Luckily, there was a band playing at the amphitheater. There's almost always something going on. Even if it is just happy hour, it's a good place to get liquored up. Thank God for internet ride-share. Vee and I had just a little too good of a time on Valentine's Day. We ended up sleeping it off. We both ordered Bloody Marys for breakfast, to go with our bloodshot eyes. We missed the sunrise, and I sure don't want to miss another one, especially with Vee. The water was a bit nippy for us. But the snowbirds were jumping right in. They certainly didn't need wetsuits.

We seem to be at an impasse over adoption. I can't get past the cost. It isn't like there is a shortage of prospective parents. Maybe we should consider adopting a child from the foster care system. More than likely, the child would be walking and talking a lot! Raising a toddler. Instant family. According to Walter, there is a great need, though, especially for minority children. I don't think I could deal with that bureaucracy. Walter said it was a red tape nightmare. I just don't know what to do.

Chapter 11:
Goodbye, Dad

We cruised back in town, Monday around 3 p.m. I went over to pick up Tiki and took her home. I just finished feeding her when my phone started to buzz in my pocket.

"Hi Mom, how was your weekend?"

"Will, Dad just had a heart attack. They are taking him to Savannah Central Hospital. They have the best Cardio-Pulmonary unit in the city. He is in the ICU. The doctors want to talk to me right away. Can you come pick me up here at the house? I can't find his living will."

"I'm leaving right now. Dad's living will is in the safe behind your portrait. The combination is your birthdate backwards and the number six."

"Will, how do you know all this?"

"Unbeknownst to everyone, Dad made me the executor of his will. I will be there in a few minutes." I picked up Mom and called Vee en route to the hospital. She called everybody else. The doctor was waiting for us in his room. The scenario wasn't good. Basically, we had two choices. Leave Dad the way he is with a 95% blockage, and put him in hospice, or open him up and perform a quadruple bypass. The surgeon was confident that the operation would help. Men in their 80s take longer to recover, but he has a good chance. We had to decide whether to treat Dad or comfort him. The ICU team will continue post-surgery treatment. Hospice care will make him comfortable the moment they take over. Mom chose to do the bypass based on the doctor's recommendation.

Now all that is left to do is sit on our hands and wait. Mom and I sat in the surgical waiting area for an update from the surgical team. Hours passed, and there was no word from anyone. By that time, Roger, Carson, Vee, Melissa, and Katherine were with us in the waiting area. I loved seeing almost all my siblings again. I just wish the circumstances were different. Beatrice was the only one not present. She is stationed halfway across the country in Kansas. You have got to go where the Army sends you, most of the time. I sent her a text, but I haven't heard anything back yet. If she is on a mission, that will take priority over personal matters. I hope she checks in with me soon.

The double doors swung open, exposing the corridor leading to the Operating Rooms. Two members of Dad's surgical team came out to give us an update on his status. I could tell from their body language that it was not good news. They went right up to Mom.

"Mrs. Burrows, I'm sorry to inform you that your husband did not survive the surgery. He expired about ten minutes ago; what we concur with was congestive heart failure. Phillip was asleep, under anesthesia, when he died. He probably slipped away from us peacefully. Please accept mine and my entire staff's sincere condolences at this time." At this point, the entire family is crowded around Mom, crying with her. My phone started buzzing. It was Bea calling me back. I stepped away to another quiet section of the waiting room.

"Bea, I have bad news, Dad just expired on the operating table about fifteen minutes ago. He died of complications from his heart attack early this morning. Everybody is here with Mom."

"Okay, thank you for letting me know. Please give Mom my love. I will put in for emergency leave after I get off the phone with you. Can I say a word to Mom?"

"Yes, let me hand her the phone."

"Mom, can you hear me, okay?"

Sobbing quietly, Mom uttered, "Hello, Beatrice, Phillip is gone, honey. It's good to hear your voice. They said he died peacefully. I hope so. Are you coming home?"

"Oh yes, I will be leaving Kansas very soon. I need to go, Mom. I love you, and I will see you very soon. I promise. Goodbye, Mom."

Mom handed the phone back to me and told everyone that Bea was coming here to be with us. I slipped back from everyone again to call the funeral home. I spoke to the director, Mr. Wells, and he assured me everything would be taken care of right away. He already had instructions for Dad to be cremated. The only thing left to do was have Mom go pick out the Urn and schedule the memorial service and reception. We decided to wait a week for the service. This would allow some of his New York and California friends some travel time if they chose to attend. Mom asked me to do the eulogy. She felt I was closer than anybody else. I told her I would be honored.

"Welcome, everyone, family and friends, to this very solemn occasion, celebrating the life of Phillip Burrows. Phillip and his wife Martha had six children: Melissa, Roger, William, that's me, Beatrice, Katherine, and Carson. Dad, with Mom's help, raised six very successful people. We have a lawyer, an engineer, an archivist, a soldier, an artist, and a mechanic. Is there a doctor in the house?" The crowd chuckled. "We don't have one of those yet.

In preparing for this eulogy, I asked myself what Dad's legacy was to us. I came up with two things. Unconditional love and great advice. (especially financial) The man was a genius when it came to financial forecasting. Dad was the least selfish person I have ever known. He believed in securing prosperity for others. I just recently found out that while he worked as a CPA and financial planner, he contributed to many local charities. That will continue due to the trust that he created.

I never knew anyone to speak an unkind word about Dad. Usually, there's always one, but not Phil. I always felt better when he and I were together. He and I were the only two in the family who liked to surf fish. We would run over to Savannah Beach and fish off the pier or from the surf a couple of times a year. I wasn't the only one; he spent one-on-one time with all of us kids. I cherished my time alone with Dad, as I'm sure you all must have. Dad and Mom are easily the most giving people I have ever met. Dad set the bar high when it came to generosity and work ethic. To me, that says a great capacity to love. We are all going to miss you."

A lovely catered reception immediately followed the ceremony. I was amazed at some of the individuals in attendance. People came from all over the country, and several flew in from Europe. I was very moved by how many lives he impacted. Many praised Dad as a financial planner, revealing fortunes they owed to his expertise. I knew he was good at his job, but not that good. I guess we will find out how good he was when we meet with the estate lawyer next week.

The eight of us, including Veronica, sat around a beautiful antique conference table in the lawyer's office. An elderly gentleman slowly walked into the room and gingerly sat at the head of the table to read us Dad's will. He introduced himself as Percival Smith Esq., then he began to read aloud to everyone.

"... I, Phillip Burrows, do hereby leave the bulk of my personal estate to my wife Martha Burrows, to include stocks, bonds, coins, antiquities, collectables, and bank holdings to the approximate sum of 42 million dollars. To my children, I leave the sum of 5 million dollars each ..."

At that point, everyone just kind of looked at each other, trying to get a handle on the moment. Mr. Smith went on to disclose the charitable trusts set up in Dad's name. That combined estimate was over 30 million dollars. We had no say in that money. Frankly, I wouldn't want to.

Mom finally intervened by commenting, "Children, your dad and I never told you very much about our parents. Both of our fathers were Wall Street investment bankers. We both inherited several million dollars when they passed away. Your father, Phillip Jr., worked/apprenticed for his dad several years after receiving his MBA prior to Phillip Sr's death in 1957. Soon after, we met, fell in love, and mutually decided to get hell out of New York. We moved to Savannah in 1958, and the rest is history. The house you were raised in was my parents' winter cottage. Your dad and I decided a long time ago that we didn't want to live an elitist, aristocratic lifestyle. That is why, with our parents' blessing, we moved further south. Will, you were spot on about Dad being a financial genius. He had clients all over the world at different points in his career. If Phil and I had chosen to do so, we could have retired billionaires. We collectively chose not to. Money is just a tool; how it gets used will justify the user's legacy. As for my substantial holdings, when I die, I plan to have half combined with Dad's charities. The rest is up to you. You are all old enough to know that money doesn't grow on trees. So, I suggest that you invest your inheritance wisely. I would not make it generally known about your windfall. Roger, don't run out and buy an Italian snot rocket again."

"Very well, I will keep my SUV."

"Well, that's my story. Any questions?" Six hands went up.

"Okay, oldest first," Melissa asked why they kept our ancestry such a secret.

"Oh, that. Your grandparents, great-grandparents, uncles, and aunts were all aristocratic society. It is the closest thing to royalty we have in this country. Dad and I decided that we wanted to give all of you a normal, or at least what we felt was a normal, upbringing. I'm not saying that all our ancestry were necessarily bad, but most of their decisions would stem from elitist values. That way of life is very public. Financial power is envied and constantly scrutinized. On the other hand, it is a very pampered lifestyle with many privileges and opportunities. Your elders wanted for nothing.

Think about this. I have read that it can be extremely difficult for a wealthy man to enter the kingdom of heaven; odds are, your dad is up there right now based on the choices he made. I consider myself blessed that I was married to the most wonderful man I have ever known. Ask yourself, did you ever want for anything growing up? I can't think of a time when any of you didn't get what you really wanted for Christmas or your birthday. You all went to the college and university of your choosing. You are all self-made individuals able to claim all your successes and failures as your own. That is as it should be for everyone, but it is not always so.

If your father and I have failed in life, then it would be the fact that as young adults he and I made a choice to remain on the edge of success which left us with an underrated legacy, according to the opportunities placed before us. In doing so, we did compromise your dreams relative to the lifestyle that we chose not to take part in. Your inheritance will not put you in aristocratic status, but the opportunity for you to secure that lifestyle for your future generations still exists.

For what it's worth, I think we had a good life. It is obvious this family was successful at finding ways to impact the lives of others. The fact remains that one or more of you could have been a major player in world politics or something along those lines. But none of you aspired to pursue that. Beatrice, would you like to be a Lieutenant General? Would any of you want that level of success?" Several shaking heads were at the table. "Any other questions?"

Roger asked, "Why did you wait until now to tell us?"

"That's another good one. I wanted to tell you individually when you turned twenty-five, but Dad didn't think it was fair not to reveal to everyone at the same time. Now I tend to agree with him on this one. It was hard enough for the two of us to keep that cork in the bottle. Okay."

"Will, how about you?"

"Was Dad ever a billionaire?"

"As a family, we got about halfway there once. The bulk of it has gone to the charity trust. It's too much money for me. I don't understand how people comprehend it all."

"Mom, now I feel guilty having all my friends paint our house for free."

"Don't feel too guilty. Those steaks they polished off were over a hundred bucks a piece. Most of them ate two."

"Good point, Mom."

"Beatrice, what about you?"

"Did Dad ever use any of his influence to secure my promotions?"

"No, every promotion you received was based on your own merits. As for the rest of you, we paid for your secondary education; after that, you were on your own. Anybody else? Good, I'm starving, let's go out for pizza and beer. My treat, of course."

We all piled into our cars and headed to Mom's favorite little Italian place, and we had a wonderful reunion. It wasn't the same without Dad, though. Mom seemed okay with his passing today. Over the weekend, I heard her crying in the bathroom. They were such a beautiful couple. It will take all of us time to fully grieve properly.

Dad never made it to hospice care. I received a flyer in the mail from the local Hospice Care facility. It mentioned grief counseling. I think it would help Mom and me both. Beatrice has more experience dealing with death than any of us. She was combat-deployed twice. I invited her over to share dinner with Vee and me. There are several questions I have for her.

Chapter 12:
Back Home, Moving Forward

I just put the Seafood Au Gratin in the oven when the doorbell rang. I asked Vee to let Bea in. I set the timer for eighteen minutes, walked over and gave Bea a big hug, then I grabbed some beers out of the fridge.

"So, Will, what are you and Veronica going to do with your 5 million dollars?"

"We have no clue. What about you?" She took a sip of beer and shrugged her shoulders.

"I guess it is a nice problem to have, now I can go to any university I want. Or, if I decide to live at home and go to Savannah University, my GI Bill will cover the first four years. I am leaning toward a nurse practitioner or medical technician. But who knows? I am also interested in social work. I hate to admit it, but having the money changes things. For the first time in my life, I don't have to decide on a career based solely on monetary gain. It may sound crazy, but I wouldn't object to owning an antique shop."

"Wow, if I didn't already work for a museum, I would go halves with you. Savannah is the place for an antique shop. You can't walk 500 yards in any direction without hitting one in this town. I'm sure there is one for sale. You could bankroll an auction house, maybe. We're getting ahead of ourselves. Get your degree first."

"Good point, brother."

Vee piped in, "There are a couple of antique shops for sale right now, but commercial real estate is booming despite the housing crash. It's weird, everyone is switching to commercial property to invest in. You might want to wait a few years and get a degree in history or library science, something with an archive background. Concentrate on investing, and give your money time to grow a bit. Wall Street is very bullish right now."

"Another good point."

"Bea, one reason I asked you over tonight was that I want to try and get Mom to get some grief counseling. You have a good bit of experience with that, don't you?"

"Yes, quite a bit, more than I care to admit, too. When I was deployed in Iraq, I lost several of my troops in supply convoys. It was such a dirty business. I noticed Mom could use some grief counseling to help her move on. They were two peas in a pod. Is it true they still liked to tear one off now and then?"

"Oh yes, I came over one evening a few years ago and caught Mom upstairs in a purple and black corset. Luckily, she didn't see me. I don't mind telling you it was very disturbing to me, because she looked really hot in that outfit. I had to go home and take a shower; I felt so dirty. It was so creepy. Thank God, she didn't see me. I slipped out of the house and came back a few hours later. From then on, I always called prior to coming over. Okay, you can stop laughing now."

"So, Will, was she wearing fishnet stockings too?"

"Yes, and six-inch heels."

"Oh boy, I always knew they were a little kinky, but wow, that is creepy to think about. Honestly, they did have six kids, so Mom and Dad had to have a pretty active sex life."

"Can we please not talk about this?" Vee walked out of the bathroom. "Talk about what?"

Bea quipped, "Mom and Dad's sex life."

"Did he tell you about the corset. He told me she was a hottie in that thing?"

"Aw, cut it out, both of you! Would you two like to set the table, please?"

"Will, I would be glad to speak with Mom about grief counseling. Lord knows it did me a world of good. I saw many of my cohorts struggle with PTSD because they wouldn't admit to themselves that they needed to talk to someone about their personal demons. We all had them. Some just dealt with them better than others. The nights were the worst. I have been ok since then. I still see a psychologist once a month."

"Bea, you are getting out very soon, right?"

"Yes, now that I don't have to worry about money, I am going to use up all my vacation/leave and get out four months early. I will be out in 126 days. 125 and a wake-up. I have been able to see many parts of the world and get paid to do it. Some parts I could have done without, but I have been there just the same. I hope that the places I went and the people I met are better off for knowing me. I do hope that is true. There was one guy I met in Germany. He was a veteran and decided to homestead there. We had lots of fun together. I spent a week with him in Minich during Oktoberfest. That was wild. If I was ever going to get married, he would have been the one. He was a barber by trade. Same old story, I was always away from the base, leading some convoy. Riley was really good to me. Sometimes I wonder what he is up to."

Vee asked, "Do you have a way to get in touch with him?"

"No, I tried contacting him a few years ago, but I had no success. I heard he relocated to South Florida to be with his family, but I was never able to find him. Will, Mom told me about the infertility thing. She said it was irreversible. I'm so sorry, I know how much you wanted to be a daddy."

"Yes, thank you. It was a blow, but I think we have learned to accept that fact. We still haven't ruled out adoption. It can take a couple of years to adopt a baby. I guess that isn't too bad. It takes nine months to make one on your own."

"You guys get to pick the sex of the baby, right?"

"Yes, we do."

"What would you want, boy or girl?" I glanced over at Vee.

"We never even discussed it. It doesn't really matter to me. Vee, what would you prefer?"

"A girl, definitely a girl."

"Okay, awesome, a daughter. Cool. I hadn't really thought about adopting a baby since Dad's death. I know he was eighty-three, but it's still kind of a shock that he's gone. The money was unexpected. Vee and I were well off before, now we have no worries at all when it comes to money. We had given serious consideration to moving back in with Mom. I'm sure Roger will be moving out pretty soon. At least I would assume so. Interesting, if we move back in, and everyone decides to stay, it might be fun having the house full again. That would be something else. I wonder what Tiki would think. It's actually a shorter commute for both of us. I wonder if that would have any bearing on the adoption process. I can't see how it would, but one never knows about these things. By the way, when are you planning to fly back to Kansas?"

"I fly back a week from today; I will try to set up some type of grief counseling with Mom before I leave. Would you two like to go down to the waterfront tonight? I haven't been down there in ages."

"Sure, I will go and get all liquored up with you, Vee. Do you want to chaperone, or should we get a ride down there?"

"I'm not driving, we can take a ride-share." After dinner, we freshened up and headed downtown. The river is always pretty at night. It wasn't too overcrowded either. There is something about those cobblestone streets, visiting Forsythe Park, and the squares all over town that says home to me. Savannah is easily one of the most romantic cities in North America. I can't forget the azaleas adorning Victory Drive; everything is saturated in pink, it's spectacular.

We got in really late. Bea crashed on our living room couch. I never saw anyone put away so much rum in one sitting. Or in her case, one slumping to one corner of the bar. She will need several Bloody Marys in the morning. The Army sure taught her how to hold her liquor. I hope she doesn't get bent like this all the time. She was probably letting off some steam. Mustering out of the service will be a huge adjustment for her. I hope it doesn't prove overwhelming. That would be unfortunate.

I think Vee was a little concerned, as I was, at how Bea was throwing down shot after shot. I have heard taboo stories about career soldiers and alcoholism. By the third bar, Bea was really hammered. It was almost 3 am. I went to bed.

The next morning, we saw Bea in the kitchen cooking eggs, bacon, sausage, waffles, and coffee. The table was set and ready to be plated for us.

I was like, "Wow! How did you survive last night? If I tied one on like you did, I wouldn't be waking up until tomorrow afternoon."

"Oh, I got up and did some roadwork, took a hot shower, and hopped in the kitchen."

Sarcastically, I quipped, "You do realize I despise you right now for being in such incredible shape."

"Sorry, brother, I tied one on pretty good last night. I don't remember much after the ride home."

"I gotta ask. You don't drink like that all the time, do you?"

"No, I think it might have been a combination of things. It was mostly Dad's passing. It hit a little bit harder than I was ready to admit. During my run this morning, I was able to sort some things out in my head. I am very glad to hear you are considering moving back in with Mom. I was worried she would be alone if Roger and Carson decided to move out. I won't be there for another few months. I am definitely going to move back in with mom. I will be discharged in mid-semester. It will give me a couple of months to decide when and where I want to go to college. I have a question. Have you had any quality time with Melissa since we came back for the funeral? I know she has never been a real chatterbox, but I would like to pick her brain a little and hear what she is up to."

"Me too. I spoke to her for a minute or two at the memorial service, but after the receiving line, she took off."

"Melissa is still working in Atlanta, right?"

"Yes, the last I heard, she had just made junior partner in the law firm she works for, but that's all I know."

"I guess we will have to drag it out of her like always. What about Katherine?"

"Katie is doing great. She wants to open her own auto repair shop. Now there will be no stopping her. It's nice having a mechanic in the family. Now, if you just go to med school, we will have a doctor in the family, too. How about it?"

"Nice try, but I am really leaning toward antiquities. I like antique weapons. I have amassed quite an extensive collection on my travels. I have many desirable and rare specimens from the Revolution, American Civil War, and WWII. It's amazing what soldiers will part with when money is tight. Then there is old Sarge to make a deal with. Some of those bums didn't have any idea what they had. The jewel in my collection is a French 17th-century matchlock rifle, along with several flintlocks. Also, a set of dueling pistols from the early 1800s. I have swords, sabers, and one complete U. S. cavalry uniform. They are all original. Some belong in a museum. I'm sure my Brown Bess flintlock does. It is gorgeous."

"Have you ever had any of your collection appraised?

"Don't bother, I know exactly what my collection is worth. It's insured for just under $200,000. I didn't have much else to do with my money, so I started by purchasing a couple of pieces from a local auction, and ten years later, I managed to put together quite a collection. I am serious about opening an antique store or purchasing one. If I stick to just weaponry, I don't really need to go back to school, but I think it would benefit me greatly to get a bachelor's in history."

"Good plan, sis. Go to Savannah University, they have a great history department."

"Yes, but they are not the only ones. There are several others I am considering. I am concerned about Mom though. That is one of the Savannah factors. When it comes right down to it, I may end up living back home for a while. I have been away for twenty years. That's a long time away from family. I only made it back home for three holidays. Two Thanksgivings and one Christmas. I really missed you guys a lot. Especially when I was overseas, I just could never get away at that time of the year. I spent many Christmases with foreign families. Most of them I really enjoyed, but it was never like coming home. Mom's kitchen always smelled so intoxicating with all that delicious comfort food coming right out of the ovens. The bedding was always fresh and cool. I would pull one corner of the sheet and comforter only slightly away from the mattress, then slip between the flat sheet and fitted sheet. I let the coolness infuse my entire body while the sunbeams penetrated through the windowpane in my room. I used to do that a lot on really hot days. I loved to sneak in a catnap for an hour before supper. Oh yeah, what happened to the tree fort? I saw it missing at the house."

"Sorry, sis, the floor fell apart, and I had to dismantle it. None of us would fit in it anyway."

"That's okay. I had my first kiss in there with Matt Jenkins."

"He told me he got to third base with you."

"Well, not that day anyway."

"Oooh, oooh, stop, la, la, la, la. TMI. TMI."

"Knock it off, you big baby. FYI, Mom invited us over for Sunday dinner. I think she just wants to see everyone one more time before we scatter again. Well, Melissa and I anyway."

Chapter 13:
The Next Generation

Vee and I pulled up in Mom's driveway. Roger was waiting at the doorstep. We walked through the door, and the smell of Chicken Parmesan overwhelmed me. I was thinking, nice. Then, I poured myself a drink and parked my butt on the couch next to Melissa.

"Melissa, what have you been up to since I saw you last?"

"I am getting married this coming June. His name is James Dowling. He owns his own manufacturing business. They make aftermarket automotive parts. He is very successful and very handsome. Here is a photo of us in Gatlinburg ten days ago, that is when he proposed."

She pulled the ring out of her purse and slipped it on her finger. The big stone was almost three carats. I didn't want to say anything at the memorial service. "He is a really nice guy, and we enjoy our lives together. He has never been married either. He told me he came really close once, but she died in a car accident six weeks before their wedding. It took him a long time to get over her, and he assumed marriage was never going to happen for him. We are almost the same age. James is exactly one month older than I am. We plan to get married in Atlanta, and he is insisting on paying for everything. He wants a big wedding. Vee, he knows your dad."

Vee asked, "How did you guys meet?"

"My law firm handled a case for his best friend. After he won the case, there was a huge party to celebrate. That is how I met James. We have been dating for a little over a year. He owns several houses and a Diner he inherited from his parents several years ago. James lives with two of the cutest golden retrievers I have ever seen, Molly and Madge. They are sisters from the same litter. He likes to hunt and fish when he gets tired of counting money. At some point, you all will have to be fitted for your wedding attire. I want you all at the wedding. James has a brother and a sister as well. We would like to have a meet and greet for the families sometime in March or April. Bea, will you be out of the service by then?"

"Can you wait until mid-May? I will be discharged and home by then."

"Sure, we can wait. I am sending your party invitations to Mom. Tentatively, we will shoot for the second weekend in May. Does that work for everyone?"

Everyone nodded. Then we all headed for the buffet line to eat.

Bea announced to everyone at the table, "I have decided to attend Savannah University to attain my degree in history. Mom, is it okay if I move back into my own room?"

"Sure, honey, I can't wait."

"I am scheduled to be discharged on May 6th but it depends on when the orders are cut. It could actually be a week earlier. I will know when they send me my orders. Then it is just a one-way ticket here. I am excited about getting out. I did my share of soldiering for the last twenty years. It's somebody else's turn now. I am looking forward to purchasing a new wardrobe. Almost everything I own is either green or khaki. I am going to need a new vehicle as well. I don't own a car right now. I meant to get one when I came back from overseas, but I just never got around to it. Actually, since arriving in Kansas, I haven't ventured off the base enough to warrant the investment. At this point, I may just wait until I get back here."

Roger spoke up and said, "Sis, you can have my SUV. It's practically brand new. I am going to get a small coup again."

"Thank you, Roger. How much do you want for it?"

"Don't worry about it. It's paid in full. We just need to get the title in your name when you return in May. It will be waiting for you in the garage."

"That is very generous of you. Thank you so much. I hope I can return the favor someday."

Roger spoke again, "That is just my way of thanking you for your glorious service to our country. FYI, starting tomorrow, I have a new job. Will, your friend Walter just hired me as his new office manager. It's not exactly engineering, but the salary and hours are great. I will basically oversee the entire operation for Walter and his wife. Walter signs the checks, but I decide whose name is on the payline. He and his wife seem like really good people to work for. It is almost an hour commute from the house, so Mom, I will be moving out as soon as I find another place." One in, one out, life goes on. I think it is definitely time that Vee and I talk to Mom about us moving in with her.

Mom asked, "Kathleen, how is the new garage coming along?"

"Very well. The building renovations should be done by the end of the month. Two more permits, and 'Kate's Garage,' we will be open."

"That's wonderful news. How many employees are you going to hire?"

"Seven or eight, I will have to see how busy we are. My shop will be the only independent facility certified to work on electric vehicles in Savannah. I see that the industry is finally taking off in the coming decade. People will eventually start buying and selling used electric cars. I will catch much of that repair business. In the meantime, I can repair everything on the road except semi-tractor trailers. I have a very good rapport with most of the dealerships in town. I should get many referrals. There are certain repairs that dealerships don't like to get stuck with. Especially if they are swamped with warranty work. I am very excited."

"Carson, how about you?"

"Now, Mom, you know I hate to talk about my work."

"Yes, but what about your art exhibit in Atlanta next month?"

"All the paintings are done. The truck is picking them up next week."

I said, "I didn't know you had a show coming up?"

"Yes, I sold four paintings at my last show, and they begged me to do another one. no big deal. Mom, I may be moving out as well. I need a bigger studio. I found a converted warehouse over in Savannah Beach that needs to be renovated. Roger, I need to talk to Walter. I would like to get an estimate this week."

"Yes, I will take care of that tomorrow morning." After dinner, Vee and I helped Mom with the dishes.

"Mom, Vee, and I would like to move in with you after Roger and Carson leave. We are seriously thinking about adopting one or two children. Would you like to have a younger generation of children living with you again?"

"Oh my, nothing would make me happier than to see you two raise a family here. I must warn you, though, my babysitting rates have gone up quite a bit!"

"That's okay. I think we can afford you."

"How soon would you receive the child?"

"It's about a two-year process; we haven't officially applied to become adoptive parents yet. One of the main things is that we would have to pass an independent home study. A social worker would have to inspect the house. This place is in immaculate condition and fully up to code. I seriously doubt there would be any issues. At this point, we would want to be moved in before starting the adoption process. We would wait for Beatrice to move in as well. Another potential babysitter."

"It sounds like the two of you have all this planned out pretty well. I have news for the two of you. When it comes to raising kids. There is no plan. No crystal ball to guide you through. The kid, or in my case, kids, show up, and that is when all the fun begins. Phil and I managed to raise six wonderful, healthy, individual personalities - each with a flair to succeed. The only ones with any sense of commonality are you and Beatrice. That's the middle children putting a new wrinkle on things. Your dad, before he passed away, told me one very chilly evening in front of the fireplace, 'Martha, we did very well, raising six kids. Not a bad one in the bunch. We managed to bring all of them to the edge of success. Thank you for being my companion through it all. I feel as close to you tonight as ever before.' That was the last night I made love to your father, which was about five months ago. I will surely miss that man, but I am so thankful for all the incredible things we shared. You will have that as well. That's the treasure that you get to keep as parents. You get to share in the successes that your children will have, and their failures as well. It just goes with the territory. Phil used to talk about tradeoffs in business. They happen in life, too. I can look back with no regrets. No tradeoffs I would not endure again for any of you. Being a parent has brought me everlasting joy."

Vee and I drove back home after talking with Mom. We sat, driving along in silence, trying to soak in all the intellect that woman just passed on to us. Dad always got the credit for being a financial genius, and he was, but Mom had the foresight and wisdom of the humanities that Dad could never realize. I forgot she is a college graduate as well. Mom has a degree in sociology. Aside from being very smart, she is keen on everything that takes place around her at all times. That takes patience and cunning. Mom certainly has both.

They were always a team when solving problems, not that there were many, but a team, nonetheless. The eight of us always communicated with one another. Everybody had their moments, but they didn't last long, because the rest would hound them so bad they wanted to get it off their chest just to stop all the constant badgering. There were never any secrets in that house, which makes it all the more impressive that Mom and Dad kept our inheritance a secret all those years.

I pulled the car into the garage and turned off the ignition. Vee reached over and gave me a very long, passionate kiss. We went into the bathroom, undressed, and hopped in the bathtub together. As I sat there enjoying the warmth and closeness of Vee's body next to mine, I thought to myself, we won't be doing this very much once the adoption goes through. Hopefully, that is not true. We will have some romantic time together. The kid has to sleep sometime. Hopefully, they go to bed early. Yes, that's it, an early bedtime.

"Cool!"

Vee said, "Honey, the water is nice and warm."

"I meant it is cool sharing this moment with you."

"Oh, that's very sweet. I love the fact that I married a passionate man. It makes my heart happy."

Chapter 14:
The Edge of Success

The following Monday morning, I called Dottie from the adoption agency and told her that Vee and I were interested in moving forward with the adoption process. Dottie requested a follow-up appointment to discuss the process in more detail. I told her that I would have Vee call her back with our availability.

I headed back over to Mom's to take a few measurements for the new nursery. I guess that is all I can do in the form of prep right now. Any baby furniture purchases will have to wait until the blessed day approaches. I asked Mom where all of the old baby stuff ended up.

"Will, everything got packed away and put in the attic. When you moved up there, I don't know where it ended up."

"When Dad and I emptied out the attic, all that stuff ended up in the attic over the garage."

"Yes, son, that's right. Sorry, wrong attic. Why do you want that stuff? You should buy all new furnishings."

"We plan to, but I would like to restore the bassinet and cradle."

"Yes, definitely the cradle. That thing goes back several generations."

"Mom, do you ever talk to any of your New York relatives?"

"I do write my cousin, Anne Grayson, every year. We have been corresponding with each other since almost the time Phil and I moved to Savannah. It's usually around the holidays and doesn't amount to much more than a salutary family Christmas letter."

"Was there ever a suggestion to reunite with them?"

"No. Our families live in two different worlds separated by a catastrophic fortune. Your father, God rest his soul, made sure any financial dealings we had with his and my extended family were of a business nature. It was always strictly business."

"Why was Dad so important to their business?"

"Your father had many worldwide contacts. He acted as a liaison for other family members. Some I approved of. Some I didn't. Don't worry, we're not going to get a phone call from Interpol or the IRS. It was mostly the way that his cousins would be so friendly one minute and curt the next. They didn't want Phil to retire. He finally told them to take their money elsewhere. That was a great day for us. The financial freedom it gave us was beneficial, but in the end, half of that money ended up as charitable contributions. That I liked. Your dad insisted that a portion of the income he generated for them had to be put in his foundation. Also, it had to be anonymous. His cousins hated that, but that was the only way Phil would help them. It actually gave everyone a nice tax shelter. Your old man was a very smart cookie, and the kindest, most sincere gentleman I've probably ever met."

"So, Paul Brentler was just a summer romance."

"Paul was my first love in high school. First kiss, first everything. Paul was sweet, but a little impetuous. He was very gentle and patient with me that first time."

"Eeww, Mom, don't talk about your sex life with me!"

"Oh, don't be so bashful, I don't imagine you and Vee hang out in the kitchen baking cookies for Sunday school class every night."

"Okay, you got me there. We are very passionate with one another. That is why not being able to conceive children is so devastating to me."

"Will, I would love to tell you that life is candy-coated moon beams and caldrons of gold at rainbows' end, but life is not that simple. You and Vee can attempt to live a simple life, but it won't be any less stressful. If college taught me anything, it is that stress, or change, is a consistent part of the human social experience. Change is inevitable, and my sweet child, surviving all of life's difficult times depends on adaptability. Disappointment is not the end. It is an opportunity for growth. You and Vee have enriched each other since the first day you met. I guess what I am trying to tell you is, don't let infertility destroy your path beyond the edge of success."

As I sat there in Dad's old lounge chair, I contemplated my mother's wisdom. I know she is right. Life is not cotton candy and carousels. I have to put disappointment behind me and trust in my ability to move on.

I drove back home that Saturday afternoon feeling a little bit wiser for the journey. I pulled into the garage and remembered Vee is having a girls' night out, so it is just Tiki and me tonight. I walked through the door, and Tiki was right at my feet to greet me. We both strutted our way to the kitchen. I opened a can of pate for her, and she put it away in short order. There is nothing wrong with that cat's appetite. I grabbed a steak out of the fridge and put it in a hot buttered skillet. I accompanied the N. Y. Strip with a few stalks of asparagus and turned on the TV. I changed my routine tonight. Beer, steak, TV, then I ended up dozing off on the couch watching a baseball game.

I woke up an hour later with Tiki sitting right in front of me.

"What is the matter, Tiki?"

As if I couldn't guess, time to scoop the litter box. I got up and grabbed the pooper scooper and ran it through the litter box. Tiki immediately hopped in and took care of business. Then I scooted down the hallway to take care of business myself. Lately, I have been having a little discomfort urinating. I might have a urinary tract infection. I'd better get checked out. I glanced over at the time. Almost 11 pm, Vee must be having a good time out with the girls. Speak of the devil, there she is pulling into the garage now. Vee ran through the door on her way to the bathroom. She appeared from the bathroom with a very relaxed look upon her face.

"How was your night out with the girls?"

"Well, I mostly listened to the other girls bitch and complain about their immature boyfriends. I told them to stay the hell away from you, or I would scratch their eyes out and feed them to Tiki. Honey, how long has it been since I told you how much I love and appreciate you?"

"I don't know, it couldn't have been more than two or three days ago. I know you forgot yesterday. It's okay, I'll let you slide on that one. So, your friends are struggling in their relationships. What has them so perplexed?"

"It's the same old stuff. Trust, financial, and commitment issues seem to be a very recurring theme with all of them."

"Vee, it sounds like they are looking for Mr. Right and spending time with somebody else. Maybe they enjoy being able to complain about them."

"No, I think it's mostly an unwillingness to communicate. They're just lonely. Two of them are divorced, so you would think that they would know better, but no, they don't seem to have a clue. I feel bad for them not being able to find a trustworthy man to spend time with. They are all successful career-oriented women like me. Will, I don't think you realize how uncommon our relationship is. We met the old-fashioned way, face to face and not in a bar, singles club, or on the internet. Sometimes I feel like there is nothing we can't survive together. Well, right now I need a hot shower. Care to join me, stud?"

"Sure, any time, my love."

Chapter 15:
The Hardest Wait

Monday morning found me waiting in line to give a urine sample at the doctor's office. I called first thing, and they told me to swing by. Then I headed off to work. I am glad I called because I am experiencing more discomfort during urination. Hopefully, it is just a UTI like I thought.

When I got to work, it was the same old chaos. Shawn just booked three new traveling exhibitions for next month. That means I will be very busy for the next few weeks. I feel good about where we are in preparation for these upcoming events. We should be fine. My phone started buzzing again. It was the doctor's office.

"Hello."

"Hi, Mr. Burrows, this is one of the nurses at Dr. Payne's office. We would like you to come in for some follow-up bloodwork. Can you come in some time this afternoon?"

I took a little personal time and went over to the office. They drew a few vials of blood and told me they would have the results of the cancer screen in a couple of days. Cancer. Why is it always cancer? I guess I will have to sit on my hands for a few days until the results come in. Should I tell Vee now or wait? I'd better tell her now. I called Vee and she answered on the first ring.

"Hi honey, what's up?"

"Vee, I just left the doctor's office again. They asked me to come in for a cancer screening. I gave them a blood sample and was told the results would be available in a few days. I have a consultation with Dr. Payne on Thursday morning. I hope it is nothing. I am headed for home."

"Honey, I just got home. What do you want for dinner?"

"Surprise me."

I walked in the door to the smell of Chicken Parmesan. I kissed Vee and headed right for the bathroom.

I came out of the bathroom, and a drink was waiting for me at the dining room table. I sat down and began to sip on my "Rusty Nail."

Vee asked me, "Will, were you ever exposed to asbestos in your construction days?"

"Yes. I thought about that too. I was definitely exposed, but I always wore the mask and the suit for protection. Of course, that's the exposure that I know about. I could have been unwittingly exposed. That might explain my infertility. It is going to be a long three days. I do know this. We are going to go to Hawaii for vacation this February."

Vee prepared a delicious dinner; the chicken was absolutely perfect. Better than Monty's. It definitely took my mind off the blood test. Well, that, and a couple more "Rusty Nails." I was just going to have to sweat out the next few days the best way I know how.

Thursday morning finally came, and I found myself sitting in front of Dr. Payne listening to him explain the results of my blood test.

"Will, it is definitely Testicular Mesothelioma. You are looking at around five years, maybe longer. There are breakthroughs all the time. Keep your chin up. I recommend that you start treatment with a specialist immediately."

"Doc, this is the reason I am sterile, right?"

"Maybe, but there were no indicators or symptoms to corroborate that when you were tested. I'm so sorry. You are going to have a fairly rough road ahead. But look, people do survive this."

"What treatments are available?"

"Surgery, followed up with radiation therapy, is the most common treatment."

"Will surgery mean removing my testicles?"

"There is a very good possibility you could lose one or both, depending on your level of infection. I am sending you to Dr. Selton. He is a good man, and you can trust him. He can give you more answers than I can. Please keep in touch with my office. Take care."

I left the office feeling like less of a man than before. How are you supposed to deal with the likelihood that your nuts are going to end up in a jar? This has to be related to my infertility. What about an erection? If this pain in my groin gets much worse, I won't care about getting a hard-on.

I got an appointment with Dr. Selton in two weeks. I was very fortunate for a cancellation. It was originally six weeks. Vee has been so supportive. Most nights, we just snuggle together for a while. It feels good to know I am loved. So far, it hasn't interfered with work. I told Shawn about my diagnosis. She was also very understanding. If I do have to have surgery, I will probably have to take a medical leave. I'm sure it would be approved.

The two-week wait to see Dr. Selton was frustrating. Not really knowing what to expect weighed heavily on me. The blessed day came, and he was finally in his office. After examining me and performing more blood tests, he recommended removing both testicles, followed by radiation treatments to keep the cancer under control. Not what I wanted to hear. Dr. Selton scheduled my surgery for Friday of next week. I asked him if I would be able to have sex after the surgery, after both testicles were removed.

"Will, that is based on the individual. Some men never have any performance issues, some need a testosterone boost, and others lose all desire for sex. I hate to say it like this, but it really is a numbers game. Three out of four men achieve some sort of normalcy in that department. That is the relatively good news. Now, I have got to be brutally honest and tell you most men in your situation don't live more than six years after diagnosis. I say most men. Routine screenings after the surgery can help you find any recurrence. Right now, we need to concentrate on the surgery. Then we will follow up with radiation treatments. I am truly sorry, but you still have time to expand your quality of life, just not as long as you expected."

"Thank you for being totally honest with me. If those numbers hold up, I will still have time with my family. I guess I will see you in a little over a week." I stopped at the nurse's station to get instructions concerning prep for the surgery. Then I went over to my mom's house. I told Mom what the doctor told me. She cried for a bit. Why does God make some parents bury their kids? I'm the one with cancer, and she is the one who has to suffer watching me die right in front of her.

"Will, did they ever say how you got cancer?"

"Most likely, I got it through exposure to asbestos. Like I told Vee, I always wore the required protection, but I got it anyway. Just unlucky, I guess."

"Son, Melissa doesn't think so. You could seek legal action if you so desired."

"I don't need the money. That's the least of my worries. At least I have time to get my affairs in order. The first thing I am going to do is go home and hug Vee for quite a long time. Then Vee and I are going camping for a few days. The surgery is a week from Friday, and Savannah Beach is lovely right now."

"Will, why don't you find a condo over there. You know you want to."

"That is a good idea, Mom. Okay, we'll go see one of those realtors while we're over there."

Vee and I made an appointment with Wentworth Realty. Jerry Wentworth showed us five condos. None of them were listed for less than half a million dollars. Well, I can't take the money with me, and the view is incredible. We made an offer on the highest listing and got it for twenty percent less than the asking price. It's all ours, bought and paid for. Even Tiki likes it. I will miss camping, though. It is nice having an indoor shower, though, and a bed with clean sheets.

I have taken to getting up early these past few mornings. Tomorrow is surgery day. I know my surgeon, Dr. Selton, tells me that everything will be fine, but he's not the one literally getting his balls cut off. That is some scary shit, no matter how I slice it. No pun intended. If Vee wasn't with me, I would be a mental wreck.

I sat down on the sidewalk in our driveway. About ten minutes later, Vee walked out and joined me on the pavement.

"Will, are you thinking about tomorrow. You are going to do fine. Soon you will be barking behind me, doggie style in no time."

"I hope so. Baby, I'm scared to death. What if they open me up and I am too far gone to help?"

"No way, your numbers would indicate that. You're gonna be okay. I have a good feeling about this. Dr. Selton has a good reputation. He's one of the best in Georgia at what he does."

"Yes, I know he is very good, and I probably have nothing to fear, but I'm still scared shitless. Well, in my case, nutless." We both started laughing.

"They do have prosthetics. Chances are you will forget they aren't real."

"True, but it will be bizarre walking around with a set of plastic balls in my scrotum. Okay, let's go cook some breakfast." Vee threw some eggs and bacon on the grill. It's hard to be depressed at the smell of sizzling bacon.

The next morning, Vee drove me to the surgical pavilion. The nurse escorted both of us right in and started prepping me for the procedure. About an hour later, the operating nurse came and took me to the OR. Dr. Selton was waiting for me. The gas passer put the mask over my face, and I was unconscious in a matter of seconds. I woke up in the recovery room. Vee was holding my hand. She told me the surgery went very well. They got everything. That was good news. I immediately fell back to sleep. The next time I woke up, I was sitting up in bed. The nurse asked how I was feeling.

"I am a little sore down there, but otherwise okay."

"Mr. Burrows, as soon as the surgeon fills out your release paperwork, you can return home."

"Okay."

Chapter 16:
Ten Days in Paradise

The first few weeks of radiation treatment went well. Not too many side effects. A little fatigue. I decided to shave my head in lieu of watching it fall out. The doc told me I probably wouldn't suffer significant hair loss outside the affected area. I did it anyway. Actually, Vee likes it. I think she might have a thing for bald guys. She constantly rubs it when we're in bed. So far, no symptoms of erectile dysfunction, thank goodness. I'm going in for a blood test this week, hopefully it's good news.

Vee decided to go with me to hear my results. We sat down in the doc's office, and he read the results. I showed a slight improvement, and nothing in the lymph nodes. The results were vaguely optimistic.

As the treatments continue, I am feeling a lot more fatigued. I am glad there are only two weeks left. Vee gave her notice at the bank to take care of me full-time. I think she just wants to maximize the time we have left together. We booked our vacation to Hawaii next month. It will be a nice distraction while I recover from the treatments. So far, my numbers are steady, but if the cancer reaches the lymph nodes, things could get complicated. Dr. Selton said we shouldn't be concerned about that for at least a year. He isn't worried at this point, but I am a bucket of frayed nerves every time I go for test results. It's the big unknown that is the worst. Just waiting around for the other shoe to fall off. Doc told me to go to Hawaii and have a good time. That is exactly what I plan to do with Vee. We will finally see for ourselves what all the fuss is about. I definitely want to do some fishing.

We decided to take a limo from Savannah to the Atlanta airport. The first class to LAX and Honolulu. I like traveling first class. Less drama and shorter lines. We arrived at the Honolulu airport just before sunset. It was a very comfortable seventy-three degrees with a nice steady breeze. Just like the travel brochure said, it will probably rain tomorrow.

Our hotel suite was on the ocean side. I thought our view of the beach in Savannah was incredible, but it couldn't touch this place. White sandy beaches and coconut palms everywhere. The flight was very long, but it was definitely worth the effort. Beautiful as this place is, it is very difficult to forget what I have waiting for me back home. The entertainment, spectacle, landscape, and hospitality are a welcome distraction, but it's not quite enough to make me forget that I am dying of cancer. For Vee's sake, I put on a happy face and dwell on the here and now, which is breathtaking. We have another ten days in paradise before reality hits us full throttle again. I walk down to the hotel lobby to buy a newspaper, and I see other patrons pass by me. They are clueless to my inevitable fate. Elderly couples on a second honeymoon, mommies and daddies escorting the kids to the beach, young business executives, newlyweds, etc., all here for the trip of a lifetime, as are we as well.

The supposition of my story is, I will not be leaving a legacy. The best I can hope for is to secure as many meaningful relationships as possible before my time has passed. Vee, my sweet companion, will find worthiness in my memoirs. My body will return to chaos from which it came, but I will not let this be my labelled demise. My morbid thoughts shall bow to my aesthetic surroundings. I must cherish these palisade memories, promise to love, laugh, and frolic with Vee to the very end, for it would seem futile to let this happiness just slip away.

I returned to our room. Upon entering, I saw Vee stepping out of the shower and into her bathrobe. I wrapped my arms around her, pressing myself firmly against her. I kissed those soft, supple lips. She undressed me quickly and wrapped her arms around my waist. We simultaneously fell over onto the center of our king-size bed. We engaged in more amorous kissing, touching, and fondling until well after sunset. We ate room service for almost three days. The maid staff must have thought we were on our honeymoon. The next morning, we finally ventured outside together for a walk on the beach. I suggested some offshore fishing. That was a blast. We attended the hotel luau that night. I don't know what they put in those pineapple drinks, but they sure do go down smooth. For the next few days, we were recognized as tourists, complete with grass skirts and coconut bras. This tribute to my gleeful appearance will evaporate like water on the dunes. Smiles shall turn reticent during the flight home.

I feel the essence of my own seduction will eventually make me start to fade into the distance. This persona that I have tried to create is not at all what it seems. My friends and family will mourn my passing, dwelling too much on how I was struck down way too soon. I am the luckiest in this endeavor, due to my forced inevitability in accepting the fact that life is sometimes like a bucket of puss hanging over a familiar doorway. Now my days are spent in anticipation of the inevitable. I have no recourse but to accept the grief my loved ones will endure. If I could, I would take their suffering to my grave.

The last night in Hawaii, we dined at the Tiki Bar on the beach. These memories I will gladly keep close to my heart. Vee's warm, intoxicating smile will belie thoughts of a grieving family until my ultimate goodbye. As we boarded the plane and occupied our first-class accommodations, I peeked out the window to watch a magnificent sunrise. The captain came over the loudspeaker, wishing everyone a smooth journey back to LAX. Then the flight attendants got in on the act, spouting to me about how to successfully obtain and use the flotation devices. None of them knew that if I faced a decision to exit the aircraft surrounded by the ocean, I would choose not to don a life preserver and allow my body to sink deeper and deeper into the abyss. Thus, assuring myself of a burial at sea.

Chapter 17:
Cherished Moments

Twilight saw us landing safely on the tarmac at Atlanta Airport. Another luxury limo ride back home, and our second honeymoon was over. I opened the door from the garage; Vee and I were overwhelmed by a commanding chorus of "Surprise!!" The entire family was waiting for us at our condo, including Beatrice. I assumed she was retired from the Army. I was correct. Everyone was very glad that my cancer was in remission so far.

Melissa introduced me to James. "Vee, Will, I would like you to meet my fiancée, James."

James grabbed our hands and said with a smile, "It is wonderful to finally see both of you. Welcome home from Hawaii. How was your vacation?"

Vee jumped in and said, "Wonderful, fantastic, outstanding, marvelous, fantastic, just fantastic. The sunsets, beaches, booze, breezes, palm trees, everything was over the top."

I was glad to hear her say those words. This party was just what I needed to help me realize I am not alone. Many people care a great deal about my welfare. I will remember that in the coming days, months, and years to come.

I asked James how his business was doing.

"The auto parts business is doing pretty well, and the diner is super busy right now. I hired a chef to take over the kitchen, and she is amazing. The new gourmet menu is doing extremely well. We are getting some very favorable press. Now we are packed for breakfast, lunch, and dinner. Mom and Dad would be shocked at how busy we are now. Don't get me wrong, they did very well serving up eggs, bacon, grits, and BLTs for years. We still use Mom's original pancake recipe. She always said water was the secret key ingredient to superb pancakes. Thousands of flapjacks later, she was right. You and Vee should stop by sometime and try some on the house."

"Thank you, James, we will surely do that very soon. Your wedding is rapidly approaching. How are the plans coming along?"

"Very well. Thank goodness for wedding planners. Melissa and I want a simple ceremony. Just family and a few close friends. I heard your wedding was beautiful."

"It was, thanks to our very talented wedding planner. They can make a big difference. How do you like living in Atlanta? I always found it a bit too metropolitan for my taste. I have to be near the ocean."

"Will, you are right, Atlanta is a southern metropolis, complete with rush hour traffic jams, overcrowding, and a hectic pace at times, but the city is connected to everything. Especially the airport. We can get a direct flight to almost anywhere from there. Melissa and I flew to Seattle for coffee a few weeks ago. We also visited the Space Needle. It was a very nice four-day weekend. I have a cabin in the Blue Mountains, on Lake Lanier. We escape up there quite a bit. You like to fish. Why don't you and Vee join us next weekend? There's plenty of room, and I have enough fishing gear for everyone."

Vee walked up beside me, and I asked, "Vee, you don't have plans for next weekend. James just invited us to his cabin on Lake Lanier. We don't have any obligations that weekend, do we?"

"No, honey, I am still catching my breath from the Hawaii trip."

"Great, I will text you the address. It's about a five-to-six-hour trip, depending on traffic and the number of stops you make."

"Okay, should we drive up Friday or Saturday?"

"You can meet me there any time after 12pm on Friday. That will give us time to slip out on the lake that afternoon. The Bass fishing is good right now."

I was a little hesitant to try and take Tiki back to the kennel. I don't think she likes that place very much. Pets are not accustomed to coping with unfamiliar surroundings. Especially after she was just there for two weeks during our trip to Hawaii, it was unavoidable, though. James is highly allergic to cats and some dog breeds.

Vee wanted to drive up to Lake Lanier instead of renting a limo. I was okay with it, since I have had to cut back on my alcohol consumption since post-surgery. Why rent the limo if you can't raid the liquor cabinet? Actually, the drive up I-16 was nice. There wasn't much traffic once we got out of Savannah. Nothing but southern pines all along the landscape. The journey took just under five hours. Vee has kind of a lead foot in that big pickup of hers. James and Melissa were sitting on the elevated deck attached to the side of the cabin when we drove up. They had a spectacular view of the lake. I could see a big bass boat tied up to their dock. This guy knows how to live. I thought we had money. This guy must be loaded.

The log cabin was two stories, with a walk-in basement. James told me the place was just over 7500 square feet if you include the basement. I know it was tacky of me, but I couldn't help but ask. Five bedrooms, five bathrooms, a huge kitchen, two bars, one upstairs and another downstairs beside the pool table. He had a jukebox and three pinball machines. Surprisingly, no TV. It was perfect. When he and Melissa come up here, they really get away from all the hubbub. I guessed the cabin was sitting on around five to six acres. I was blown away. It was almost as nice as our honeymoon suite in Yellowstone. The only thing missing was the snowcapped Rocky Mountains in the background. James and I hit the lake in his boat around 3 pm. We trolled for a while and caught a few nice Bass for dinner. We headed back in, and I joined Vee sitting on the deck. Vee told me the master bathroom was as big as our garage. This place is overwhelming. One thing is for sure. There is a lot of money in auto parts and diners. James is also a chef and a sommelier, with an MBA as well. Oh yeah, and he's a really nice guy too.

James brought the food out to us, and I asked him, "When are the fun police going to arrive and arrest us for enjoying ourselves too much?"

"They usually cruise the neighborhood about 10 pm." We all laughed. Then, we began to enjoy our dinner.

I had to comment, "James, this place is pristine, just beautiful."

"Yes, Melissa and I really enjoy escaping the rat race up here. She kind of freaked out on me when she discovered that I didn't have a TV."

"Yes, I think my exact words were, 'Jim where is the fucking television?' Lucky for him, dinner was absolutely scrumptious. I got over it fairly quick. Fortunately for him, I have my tablet and smartphone, my lifelines to civilization."

I intervened with, "James, that dinner was delicious, but I am dying to try out that pool table of yours."

"Sure, help yourselves. I will join you in a moment after I load the dishwasher. Go ahead and pour yourself a drink from the bar downstairs. There is water, soda, fruit juice, beer, and wine, of course. The snacks are in the cabinets above."

I walked downstairs and poured myself a virgin sea breeze. Then I racked them up for 8-ball. James scampered down the stairs and told me to go ahead and break. I broke and made nothing. James proceeded to run the table on me. James dropped the 8-ball on the break. I didn't get to shoot again until the third rack. I am wondering to myself if there is anything he doesn't do well. Melissa and Vee walked downstairs and joined us. James sat behind the bar and poured drinks. He let the three of us play for a while. Apparently, James' grandfather owned a pool hall in Atlanta. Much of his youth was misspent there. I asked him if he ever considered going pro.

"I could have. I finished second on purpose in a local U.S. Open qualifier. At the time, the sport was saturated with counterculture. It was just too many vices for me. I dumped the last match to keep my amateur status. Once you turn professional, your hustling days are over. I was dating my former fiancée at the time, and I didn't want to go on the road alone. Despite how things turned out, I made the right decision. I like where my life is right now, especially with Melissa. She is wonderful and super smart. I wish I had met your dad prior to his passing. Phillip must have been an amazing guy to have left such a great family legacy."

"Dad was incredible. I miss him terribly, especially right now in dealing with my cancer struggles. I could use his sage advice again."

"Will, as far as I am concerned, you have certainly picked up the gauntlet in his place, because you seem to have everything well in hand, despite the cancer. You have been in remission for several months now, right?"

"Yes, my numbers are not perfect, but they are holding steady, thank God. The trip to Hawaii helped me sort out a great many things that were weighing very heavy on my mind. I have decided to cherish the time I have left. Mostly because that is all I can do. My doctor is cautiously optimistic about my future. So, I will follow his advice and remain positive. For

Vee's sake, if nothing else. I love her so much it hurts. I do worry about how Vee will cope after my eventual passing. I, being a few years older, assumed that I would die first. I just didn't expect it to be quite so soon from now."

"I can't say I know exactly what you are going through, but when my former fiancée, Paula, died, I thought seriously about taking my own life. I was hurt, scared, mad, and really pissed off that God took her from me. The reason I didn't kill myself was that I wanted to spite God. I did not want to give Him the satisfaction of condemning me to hell. How screwed up was that. I was not expecting to find anyone who touched my heart the way Paula did.

Then, about three years ago, I went on a blind date with my cousin's friend. Her name was Alice. I was unaware that my loving family hired me an escort. They couldn't stand the sight of me moping around like a lost puppy dog anymore. I kind of figured it out when she told me she lived in a hotel. Alice, if that was her real name, proceeded to provide me with several happy endings that night. I guess it was just what I needed, because I started dating for real, soon after that. Then I met your sister, and that was that. In my case, the blind date I went on may have been the equivalent of your Hawaii trip." I asked Melissa what she thought of his blind date.

"It was way before he met me, and he used a condom. Also, we have both been screened for any STDs. As far as I am concerned, it is a non-issue. Jim is well aware that if I ever find Alice's phone number in his contacts, well, let's just say he won't be happy after I return home from shopping with his credit card. The one with no spending limit. Right, Jim."

James muttered a very quiet and condescending, "Yes, dear. Would anyone like another drink? I could use one myself right now."

"Vee, how is your bank holding up during the post-banking crisis transition?"

"I am okay. There was an initial shakeup in the finance department. That was true with all the big banks. Most of them just started rolling up their sleeves and dealt with all the foreclosures. Melissa, your firm drew many new clients requesting bankruptcies, is that right?"

"Yes, we did, no one was immune to the financial collapse. It wasn't limited to homeowners. Small businesses got slammed as well. I am still processing bankruptcies right now. Thank goodness, there does seem to be an end in sight. The thing that disturbs me the most is all the foreclosure turnovers that are taking place. People are broke and have to sell out or get wiped out. Many have to start over with nothing, and most are relatively young in their late 30s and early 40s. Now these families are paying rent again. The opportunity to pass on wealth through household equity from one generation to the next is disappearing. This also puts pressure on personal savings and disposable income."

"You are absolutely right. I used to see it every day at the bank. Former homeowners come in assuming they have the same credit rating as when they purchased a home before, only to find out they don't qualify due to low credit ratings, lack of a down payment, and no liquid assets to use as collateral. Sorry, I didn't mean to get on a soap box, but I feel really bad for the families that come in and have their dreams crushed right in front of them."

James retorted, "I find it just a bit ironic that it was the banking industry that caused all this hardship. They created all those band-aid loans and bought and sold them like they were extreme low risk. It was just a matter of time before the housing bubble popped. It came down to nothing, but good old-fashioned greed supplemented by deregulation of the banking industry. Everybody got way too greedy, and it came back to bite them on the ass. Unfortunately, it took a great many hardworking families down with them. Now I am on a soapbox."

I commented, "Dad told me that it affected the world markets too, but not to the extent of the U.S. Economy. It took several years before prime interest rates started to rise over 1%. Economists kept throwing around the term stagflation. I never did think that deregulating Wall Street was such a good idea. Dad really hated what Washington, D.C., was up to at the time.

Okay, people, we have beaten this dead horse long enough. Does anyone want to play cards or a board game? Does everyone know how to play Canasta?" I got three nods. "Good, will get the cards." The four of us played for a couple of hours. I like James. He is good medicine for Melissa. They seem very happy together. I am glad they don't want a huge wedding like ours. It was beautiful, but it was way over the top for my taste. I did appreciate the open bar, of course.

We left for home around noon on Monday. I hope I get to stay up there with them again. That was one of the best weekends I have shared in quite a while. We arrive back just in time to pick up Tiki from the kennel. She was happy to see us. I was happy to get back to the condo and occupy my favorite chair on the balcony. I left a mountain sunrise this morning, only to be greeted by a breezy beach sunset. Vee joined me on the patio.

"Will, would you like anything to eat or drink?"

"I would love a glass of iced tea, thank you, honey."

"Sure, coming right up." I sat back and allowed myself to ease into a Zen-like state of conscious meditation. Feeling every part of my body morph into the sea foam. Inch by inch, starting with my toes and cresting at the top of my head. I am completely at peace with my surroundings. No doctors, no tests, no results, no cancer, just free to live in the infinitesimal moment. Vee caressed my shoulder, disrupting my meditative state.

"Here is your iced tea, sweetie. I love it here. Nothing to think about, but wind, sand, and waves. I feel the breeze press against my skin, making me feel alive in the moment.

Will, I owe all my happiness to you. No matter how much time we have left together, a little or a lot, I will cherish every conscious moment I have with you. You are my friend, companion, lover, the keeper of all my secrets, and the sum of all my fantasies. Thank you for choosing me to spend your life with."

"Ditto, my darling, you are the spark to my every heartbeat. I would be a vague resemblance of the man before you, without your kind, loving essence as my guide. I vow to remain the truest version of myself always."

Vee stood up and leaned over to kiss me. I pulled her onto my lap and gently pressed her head against my shoulder. I thought for a moment she was going to cry, but she caught herself and began kissing the nape of my neck. I remained reticent while she began to seduce me. I fought the urge to kiss her back. I wanted to allow my libido to be completely overwhelmed before returning any affection. Then she started to place her hand between my legs, while continuing to breathe tiny vespers along the exterior of my earlobe. I began to blink unmercifully as I began to grow severely erect. Then she slipped her hand between my briefs and me.

I stood up fully erect and kissed Vee over and over again. We dashed into the bedroom and closed the door behind us. I sat on the bed, and Vee stood in front of me. I began to undress her, exposing her lower abdomen. I placed the side of my head firmly against her torso. I began to slide my hands up and down her backside for several moments. Vee slowly ran her hands through my hair. At this point, I was ready to explode. We both slowly lay back on the bed, sharing a king-size pillow. I looked directly into those piercing eyes of hers. We began to hug each other tight and kept the embrace going for quite some time.

Chapter 18:
Cracks in the Anchor

I woke up early this morning, before dawn. I wrote Vee a note that I was going to go surf fishing and try and catch us some breakfast. I was hoping to catch a couple of nice whiting. I am of the inclination that there is no better way to start a day than a breakfast consisting of fresh fish, grits, and scrambled eggs, accompanied by coffee and cranberry juice. I grabbed my surf rod along with the rest of my gear and headed for the beach. My usual spot was completely abandoned, as usual. I flung my baited line out into the surf, placed the rod into the holder, and sat back in my chair under the shade of my portable canopy. I lay back and propped my feet up. Now all I have to do is wait for breakfast to grab my line. I like to use cigar minnows. Just about any decent-sized fish will go after them.

The seas are calm this morning. The sun is just about to crest the horizon. This is a really good way to start the day. My rod started twitching and bending. Then it went into a steady bend. Fish on! I reeled in a nice big whiting. Another one like that and breakfast is all taken care of. About two minutes later, I got another one on the line. It was a smallie. I don't keep those. I let them grow up a bit. There must have been a school that passed by. I ended up catching five more smallies. After that, the biting slowed a bit. It was still early, so I decided to stay a little longer. My patience was rewarded when I caught a nice flounder. Wow, whiting and flounder. Well, there's no sense in being greedy. I have enough filets for several meals now, and I am getting hungry. Time to head back in and stir up some breakfast. I walked in the back door, and Vee was making coffee. Perfect timing, I just finished cleaning the fish, and they were ready for the pan.

"Vee, do you want to eat out on the patio?"

"Yes, that would be lovely, honey. What did you end up catching?"

"I got a whiting and a really nice flounder. I was going to bake half of the flounder to eat for breakfast with some grits and eggs."

"That sounds awesome, baby. I have a huge appetite this morning." She sarcastically quipped, "I can't imagine why."

I started the water boiling as soon as I put the fish in the oven. People rave about prime rib and filet mignon, but I will take fresh-caught flounder and grits every day of the week. It's hard to beat good Southern comfort food.

"Will, you have another blood test coming up this week, right?"

"No, that isn't until a week from Thursday. I wanted us to go by and see Mom today, if that is okay?"

"Yes, I would love that."

"We should probably head over after breakfast. I suggest we take separate showers if we want to arrive at Mom's by noon."

"Fine, spoil my breakfast happy ending."

We finished breakfast, I cleaned up, and we headed for Mom's.

Upon arriving, we found Beatrice and Mom sitting on the front porch sharing a pitcher of lemonade. I immediately ran into the kitchen and grabbed two more ice-filled glasses. Mom makes the best homemade lemonade in Savannah. It even won a contest.

Bea announced, "Relax, Will, I made this lemonade, not Mom, but she gave me the recipe. Don't even bother asking. I will not divulge any of her secrets."

Mom interjected, "I am very glad the two of you stopped by today. My doctor wants me to have a pacemaker put in. I had been very lightheaded, so the doctor set me up with a monitoring device. Based on those results, he wants me to come in for the procedure. I was hoping that you or Vee could take me to and from the surgical pavilion."

"Absolutely, what day?"

"I need to arrive Friday morning at 7:15 am for the surgical prep."

"Oh, Friday. Darn, I'm going to the spa for a pedicure and leg wax. Sorry." General laughter ensued. "I will come pick you up at 6:45 am sharp."

"Okay, funny man, that would be very nice."

"Seriously, how long have the dizzy spells been happening?"

"For just a couple of days."

Bea said, "I noticed Mom struggling up the stairs the day before yesterday, and that is when she called the doctor. Thank you for taking Mom to the appointment. I would have done it, but I have my first midterm exam at 9 am on Friday." I asked her how college life was going.

"Between exams and getting propositioned by every guy on campus, I stay pretty busy. Some of them are really cute, but so desperate to hook up with someone. Good grief those boys are a horny bunch. I thought the Army was bad. Well, it's about the same. It certainly doesn't hurt my ego that I am still attractive to teenagers. They are probably just looking for a little MILF action."

"I used to feel the same way. I had a few classes where all the little hotties would sit in a circle adjacent to me. Then I would start flashing my wedding band, and most of them would find something to focus on."

Vee sparked up, "Most!"

"Oh, all honey! Every single one!"

"That's better."

"Vee, don't forget I can always put Charlie's wife on speed dial." Mom and Bea looked really puzzled, so we let them in on the joke. I was concerned about Mom and her dizzy spells. Hopefully, the pacemaker will alleviate the problem. Mom is no spring chicken anymore. I am so relieved that Beatrice is living with her now. That is a huge load off my mind.

I picked Mom up at 6:45 am on the day of her surgery. We arrived at the surgical pavilion, and a nurse came out with a wheelchair for Mom and took her around back. The nurse told me to wait in the lobby until she was gowned up for the procedure. Then she would come and get me, so I could wait with Mom until they were ready.

About thirty minutes later, the operating nurse came and got Mom. I walked back into the main lobby to wait until the procedure was over. As I sat there, all I could think of was how fragile she had become since Dad's passing. Hell, everyone has to die, but I will miss her terribly when she is gone. Mom is my rock. There is no scholarly confluence of wisdom that will ever replace her. She embodies the all-seeing balance of an eclectic solution for any situation: what to wear, when to arrive, what to bring, when to celebrate, and when to mourn. She shines light upon others in such a manner to benefit their current need. You can't learn that in school. It is simply the truest definition of a mother's love.

Two hours later, the doctor came and paged me in the lobby. As we walked back to the recovery room, he told me that Mom did just fine, and she is just waking up from the anesthesia. Also, as soon as she was fully awake, I could take her home. I walked behind the drawn curtain separating her from the other recuperating patients.

"Hi Will, the doc told me the procedure went extremely well. I guess this officially ends my chances of ever flying in outer space. That's okay, the food is lousy up there anyway."

I laughed along with her. Mom seemed to be her old self again. A little sore in the affected area, but nothing out of the ordinary. After the doctor released Mom to go home, we stopped at the pharmacy to pick up the pain meds that he prescribed. As I drove us back to her house, Mom kept dozing in and out on me. I pulled up the driveway, and Beatrice was waiting to help Mom up the steps and finally to her bedroom, where she proceeded to fall asleep in a matter of minutes. I walked back to the dining room table and sat down. I took a minute to relax for a moment.

"Bea, is any of that lemonade still around?"

"Yes, would you care for a glass. I made oatmeal cookies too; would you like one?"

"Sure, thank you."

Those are my favorites. I remember everyone would bulldoze down the stairs when Mom would pull a batch of cookies out of the oven. Chocolate chip, sugar, oatmeal, gingerbread, it didn't matter; they were always scrumptious. This was always such a wonderful place to grow up. Mealtimes would present the most delectable scents roaming throughout the house. Mom could make anything. Every Sunday meal was like Thanksgiving, and holiday meals were like eating at a five-star restaurant. I have been frantically searching for Mom's recipe book. That thing is probably the best-kept secret in the house right now. I even checked the file cabinets and wall safe in Dad's old office. Nothing, not even a clue where it is. I suspect that Beatrice might know. She has been doing plenty of baking since she moved back home.

"Here is your cookie and lemonade, sir."

"Thanks, sis. How do you like being back home for good now?"

"Will, I loved the service, there was always something going on. A convoy to get ready for, or some other mission. After twenty years, now I get to wake up in the morning and roll over onto the other pillow. That's pretty nice, and I get to spend time with Mom in the kitchen."

"Ah ha! You have Mom's cookbook."

"Sorry, Will, the only way I learn any of Mom's secrets is by watching her in the kitchen. She is like an artist in there. She made eggplant parmesan for us the other night. The house smelled like an Italian Restaurant for hours, and the dish was amazing."

"How is school? Are you able to keep an eye on Mom? If you need anything, just let me know. I am only a phone call away. Work has been wonderful about everything. I am thinking about retiring the first of next year. I am able to keep up the pace at work, but I usually have to take a nap for an hour or so when I get home. Then I'm okay. Eventually, I will start to feel fatigued in the afternoon at work. I will have to start training my replacement pretty soon."

"Your cancer is still in remission, right?"

"Yes, I'll go back for bloodwork late next week. I will know exactly where I am after that. I always try to be positive when I go in for tests, but it's not easy being optimistic when I get tired during the day for no reason. I have to sit down and rest for a short time before going back to what I was doing. Will you be okay with Mom now? I think I am going to head home. Thank you for the snack. The cookie tasted just like Mom used to bake."

"Yes, Mom and I will be fine. Go hang out on the beach."

"Don't be a stranger, bring Mom over and hang out anytime. I will get you an extra key to our place."

"That would be lovely, thank you."

I headed out the door and hopped into my truck, thinking Mom is in really good hands.

Chapter 19:
Vee and Me

I pulled into the garage and noticed I was home alone. I immediately headed for the fridge, grabbed a cold drumstick and a big glass of ice water. Then I went to the patio for a nice nap and snack. Tiki helped me finish off the chicken. She is always willing to lend a hand when it comes to that sort of stuff. I scanned around the beach and saw lots of foot traffic. That's a little surprising for a weekday. I should get up and join them for a walk, but I am way too comfortable right now. Besides, Vee will be home soon. She will want to know how the surgery went. I tried calling earlier, but she didn't answer. I should go ahead and thaw something out for dinner. Shrimp salad sounds good. I will get Vee to do it when she walks through the door. Tiki jumped off my lap and raced to the door. Then I heard Vee's truck pull into the garage. I walked into the room to welcome her home. She was carrying several packages. I grabbed some for her and placed them on the counter.

"Thank you, baby, I did a little clothes shopping on the way home. I had a couple of gift cards left over from Christmas. The mall was barren of customers. I had the place almost all to myself. The economy is not doing well at all right now. Several of the small stores have closed. The anchor stores are still there. I would assume that it may be just a matter of time before they start to disappear, too. More empty buildings to stare at as we drive by. It's pretty sad.

Will, remember when we were kids, and going to the mall was a social phenomenon. My girlfriends and I would meet on Saturday morning for breakfast, go to the mall when it opened, shop for a bit, and then go to the movies together. What happened to all that fun stuff? Now everything is so sterilized. Social media has replaced good old-fashioned social gatherings. I had so much fun at the paint party you organized. It wasn't just us; everybody was having such a good time. Aww, I am just getting nostalgic. We just have to adapt and move on."

"No, honey, you're right, we have lost some of our ability to socialize. I can remember just hanging out in the schoolyard at the end of the day, playing sandlot football, baseball, and basketball until sundown. That's just what we did to pass the time, and Mom didn't want us kids tramping dirt in the house until it was suppertime anyway. Everything just seems to move so much faster now. I don't necessarily think that is a bad thing. The world is a smaller place because of it. Our political ideologies from country to country don't seem to clash like they did in previous generations. I think that has to do with having faster forms of communication in place. Things aren't perfect, but half the world is not engaged in armed conflict with one another. Dad would like to talk about tradeoffs. The loss of trips to the mall for more stable foreign relations around the globe. Tradeoff, that's the ticket."

Vee retorted, "Sorry, honey, I want to hang out with my friends at the mall for a while, but I will settle for a kiss."

"You got it, sweetheart." We embraced for several moments, until Tiki started meowing and reminded us it was time to feed her. It was another world to be heard from when it comes to Tiki. I wonder who is going to die first, her or me. I guess it is a little morbid to start thinking like that. I always get a little paranoid just before I go for my blood tests. It's hard not to.

"Will, are you hungry? I can make some pasta or pork chops."

"No thanks, I am just going to go lay down for a nap."

I didn't wake up until the next morning. I made myself a cup of coffee and sat out on the patio. I am starting to realize that my life is becoming a little less sacred to me every passing day. I know it isn't healthy to look at things that way, but it is very difficult not to dwell on my impending demise. I know I should be maximizing the time I have left with my family, but I am scared shitless of going through chemotherapy. If I were faced with that option, I would seriously think about pointing a pistol barrel up against my skull and pulling the trigger. Vee walked out onto the patio.

"Hello, handsome, would you like some company?" I just smiled, and she pulled her chair right up next to mine and sat down.

She asked me, "Are you okay, sweetheart? You seem a billion miles away lately."

"I haven't been feeling good lately. My appetite is slipping, and I am feeling depressed about things right now. I have a strong feeling this next set of tests is not going to be favorable to me. Vee, I'm really scared, right down to my socks." Vee reached over and hugged me. I started weeping as my head fell into her shoulder.

"Oh, honey, I'm so sorry. You just hold on to me right now. I am going to be here for you. I want you to promise me something. Don't give up on me and your family. We are all here for you. You are never alone in this struggle. Don't forget that, mister. You heard the doctor say five years, right?"

"Yes, but."

"No buts, baby. The only butt I want you thinking of is mine when you are clenching those strong hands of yours around it in bed. Okay, so, I don't want to hear in more of this doom and gloom crap coming out of you. Got it?"

"Yes, dear." I thought to myself, God, I love my wife. Vee took me back to bed and we snuggled with each other until it was time to get dressed and head over to Monty's for dinner. Monty was not aware of my diagnosis, and there was no reason to frighten him with that bad news. He set us up at our usual table on the balcony, complete with a violin serenade. When we were finished, I asked Monty for the check.

"Not tonight, your Mom picked up the tab for you. Would you like a coffee and dessert?"

"Sure, two coffees and a chocolate cannoli."

"Right away, folks."

"Vee, you cooked this up, didn't you?"

"I told Mom we had reservations tonight; she did all the rest."

"Vee, thank you for reminding me how caring and thoughtful my family is. I was in a very dark place earlier today, but you and Mom snatched me back into the light. Thank you."

"Will, would you like to go and see a movie after we leave the restaurant?"

"Yes, I would very much like to go see a movie with you. I think this is what people refer to as a very successful married date night."

We left Monty's and walked one block over to the movie theater. I didn't even care what picture was up on the screen. I just kept focusing on Vee, kissing her hand and caressing it in mine. I dozed off a bit, leaning up against her shoulder. I guess I overdid it with dinner. She woke me up when the movie was over.

"Come on, sleepyhead, time to go home."

Chapter 20:
Tradeoffs

The doctor's office was mostly empty when I walked into the lobby. I was still very nervous and apprehensive about the impending news. The receptionist informed me that Dr. Selton was running an hour late today and asked if I wanted to reschedule.

"That's okay, I will wait." I sat down in the lobby and picked up a six-month-old fashion magazine. I looked around and couldn't even find a golf magazine. Well, I get to educate myself about New York fashion. I tried a few new colognes. They are bound to ignite a fierce passion in Vee as if she needs a reason to jump my bones. I feel very blessed in that area. I know there is no way I could deal with an impassive wife right now. I need her more than I think she realizes. Her physical affection is medicine to me. Frankly, anything that distracts me from dwelling on my cancer is a tremendous blessing. I am sure Vee knows that. She has been so strong throughout this entire ordeal.

"Mr. Burrows, the doctor just arrived. You can go and have a seat outside his office, and he will speak with you shortly."

"Thank you." I scampered down the hall and sat down. Almost immediately, Dr. Selton appeared and invited me into his office. Well, Will, you are still in remission. A couple of your numbers have dropped slightly, but nothing to be overly concerned about right now. Your appetite, libido, and attitude - how are they doing?"

"Pretty good, I get a little depressed from time to time, but Vee is a big help when that happens. I haven't suffered any erectile dysfunction or significant loss of appetite so far."

"Good, I am glad to hear that you are not feeling overly depressed. That's good, keep it up. Let's go ahead and schedule you for another screening in eight to twelve weeks. You just recently went to Hawaii, is that right? I would appreciate it if you would let me know if you plan to take an extended vacation, just as a precaution. Thanks."

"Sure, doc. I will definitely give you a call."

I left the office feeling pretty good about things. I'm still a little paranoid. I guess I have to pick my battles. I can't worry about everything. Life is chance, bedlam, and chaos all rolled into one. A guy drops his winning lottery scratch ticket in the street. He bends down to retrieve it and gets plowed into by a delivery truck. Every day is a crap shoot. Don't waste it dwelling on stuff you think might happen.

I drove back to work so that I could check up on the progress of the two new exhibits that will be opening this weekend. I walked in, and there was a message for me to meet with Shawn right away. I found her in the break room.

"Will, I am glad you decided to come back to the office. I tried calling you, but it went directly to voicemail."

"Oh, sorry, that's my fault. I forgot to turn my work phone on after I left the doctor's office. What's up?"

"Will, I have to start my maternity leave early. Sometimes, starting a family and having a rewarding career don't always mesh very well. I am having some complications due to my age. My doctor has increased my daily bed rest substantially, and there is no way I can keep working during my pregnancy. What I am not so eloquently saying is, I need you to take over my position as curator for about six months. It would be just administrative duties. You would not be responsible for any fundraising. Honestly, it isn't going to affect your workload very much. It will be a few more headaches, though. You will have to attend several more meetings. I would like to promote one of your millwork staff to shipping and receiving supervisor. Do you have a shortlist for that position?"

"Pick anyone you like; they have all run that department. I cross-trained everyone in almost every job. Even our concierge can run a power saw. That's a new position that you are looking to fill, right?"

"Yes, and it is a permanent full-time position. It is an hourly rate, not a salary. That was the best deal I could get from the Board of Directors."

"How did you cross-train all your people like that?"

"On-the-Job Training (OJT). It's nothing new. Back in my carpentry days, all my plumbers could frame, all my roofers could paint, and so on. That is how I finish on time and stay under budget. Now you know my secret."

"Wow, I always thought you were some kind of wizard with a wand and a big black cauldron.

"If that is the case, I will start advertising the position internally tomorrow morning. If you could let everyone know, I would appreciate it."

"Sure. How long do you have before you are officially on leave?"

"I have to start cutting back my hours next week. You will officially take over for me in two weeks. By the way, while you are in the role of acting curator, they are going to pay you an additional thirty-five percent of your current salary."

"Is that what you make?"

"Oh gosh, no, I make a lot more, but I do have to fundraise also. I think you are going to do fine. You are already used to carrying two phones anyway. All of my business phone calls will be routed to your extension. At this point, I mostly just put out fires that show up the same way you do. As I told you at your last evaluation, you are very good at your job. When I recommended that you take over as curator in my absence to the Board of Directors, they immediately approved. I am very relieved that you are going to be in charge while I'm out on extended maternity leave."

"Hey, wait a minute, I put out all your little fires for you already."

"I know, Will, that's why you are the perfect man for the job. Welcome to corporate politics."

"Okay, at least I know where I stand now. Shawn, you want to go to the bar down the street and order a couple of virgin daiquiris?"

"Sure, that sounds great. Call Vee, and I will call Mark; we'll make it a foursome."

We had a huge office party/baby shower for Shawn on her last day. I am happy that her leaving is on a very positive note. She ended up getting just about everything but the crib. They would want to pick that out by themselves anyway.

This kind of celebration always makes me wonder what if. What if I weren't sterile or had cancer? Would I be the one packing all of Vee's baby shower gifts in the back of her truck? Would Vee be going on maternity leave to give birth to our first child? I would be assembling our baby's first crib. I would be redecorating our spare bedroom into a nursery. I would watch Vee breastfeed our newborn child.

I had to step outside for a moment to compose myself. I just kept thinking, God has a plan for me, it may not be the plan I had in mind, but I have to face whatever lies ahead. I surely do not have to endure this much disappointment for no apparent reason. Somewhere, my suffering creates less of a burden for others. I have to believe that this is true.

Stacie came out on the patio and told me Shawn was getting ready to leave. I was asked to say a few words and give her a $500 gift card.

"Shawn, we all are so grateful for everything you do as curator here, and we will miss you dearly while on maternity leave. We want you to know that while you are away, our combined thoughts and prayers will be with you. In addition, I have been tasked with presenting you with a gift card from everyone for $500.00. That should keep you in diapers and formula for a little while anyway. Good luck!"

"Thank you so much, everyone. I will see you in six months."

Six months turned into fourteen. Then I was informed that Shawn was not returning. Apparently, the pregnancy was very difficult. That is all we were told. I tried calling Shawn, but all I got back were a few well-wishing texts.

I applied for the permanent curator position. They are still taking applications. The board knows about my cancer. To be completely honest, at this stage, I am not really enthusiastic about taking the job if they offered it to me. Most days, I am exhausted when I get home. Vee told me to resign almost a year ago, when Shawn didn't return to work after her six-month maternity leave expired. My blood tests have been slightly worse every time. Dr. Selton has discussed chemotherapy with me. I am not sure I want to go through with it. The last time I was in his office, he told me flat out I had to make a decision one way or the other about chemo. I may as well do the chemotherapy. My quality of life is starting to diminish. I am concerned about the side effects. That is a lot of poison to be putting inside my body. It looks like I will have a painful road ahead, whichever way I decide. The clock on the wall says 5:08 pm. Time to head home.

Chapter 21:
Before the Inevitable

I walked through the door and crashed on the couch for a couple of hours, like I have been doing for the last three months.

I woke up to the sound of a door closing behind me. I turned around and there was Vee hovering over me, looking dazzling as ever. I sat up and yawned with my arms outstretched. Then Vee proceeded to tease me into a tickle fight. Then we started whacking each other with couch cushions. Vee kneeled down on the floor and lay across the loose couch cushions. I dropped down beside her, and we began kissing.

"Hi Vee, how was your day?"

"It was a little vinegary. How about yours?"

"About the same. Funny, you don't taste like vinegar.

Seriously, though, I think I have decided to do the chemotherapy. You know my numbers are not getting any better. I don't really have much choice. I really hope this works."

"It will work, baby. It has to. So, what do you want for dinner?"

"How about BBQ?"

"Race you to the truck."

It was almost dusk when we got back home. I forgot to turn my phone back on when I woke up. I checked my voicemail.

"Vee, I got a call from Beatrice. Aw shit, honey we got to go. Mom is in the hospital. She had a stroke."

We bounced back in the truck and hauled ass to Savannah Central. Vee dropped me off at the entrance and went to hunt for a parking space. I scampered through the double doors and shouted, "Martha Burrows, do you know where she is?"

The security guard looked it up on the computer and said, "ICU, third floor." I hopped on the elevator and got off on the third floor. The nurse's station was only a few yards away.

"Nurse, where is Martha Burrows?"

"Are you a family member?" Beatrice poked her head out of a room down the hall.

"Will, where have you been?"

"Sorry, I had my phone turned off. We were at dinner. What the hell happened?"

"Mom had a massive stroke. She was barely alive when we got to the hospital in the ambulance. Mom is stable but not out of danger. They want to operate first thing in the morning. I wrote it down. She suffered a Hemorrhagic Stroke. Basically, an artery in her brain ruptured. They want to do some type of craniotomy. They want to cut open her skull. Will, I am so scared." We hugged for a bit.

I asked, "What time will the surgeon be here in the morning?"

"They want to start prepping her for the procedure around 7 am."

"Do you want me to stay with her tonight?"

"Sure, okay."

"Sis, can you be here in the morning?"

"Yes." Vee came into the room and sat down. Bea and I brought her up to speed.

"Will, do you need anything else from the house other than socks, underwear, and a toothbrush?"

"No, go ahead, you two, and get some sleep. I will try and do the same. I'll see you in the morning." We said our goodbyes, and I lay down on the pullout couch in Mom's room and fell asleep.

The next morning, the surgeon woke me up.

"Mr. Burrows, I am Dr. Roberts. I will be operating on your mother this morning."

"Hello, how is she doing?"

"Martha is stable, and her vital signs are good enough to go ahead with the craniotomy. This should release pressure in the affected area and allow us to repair the damaged blood vessel."

"Doc, is this her best option?"

"Yes, this procedure has the best chance for a successful recovery."

"Okay, I am going to trust your judgment on this one." About thirty minutes later, two of the surgical team members came and escorted Mom into the OR. The surgeon told me she would be in surgery for three to five hours. Vee and Beatrice brought me my hygiene items and some breakfast. I got cleaned up, and we all sat in the waiting room together. The waiting sucks. Every time someone would walk through the double doors to the operating rooms, the three of us would ogle the person until they passed by. Doctor Roberts finally passed through the door after almost four hours had passed.

"Good news, Martha's surgery went very well. We were able to make the repair, and she should wake up from the anesthesia in an hour or two. I recommend that she be transferred to a rehab/recovery facility as soon as she is physically able. Hopefully, that will be in a few days."

"Dr. Roberts, thank you so much for everything. Thank you for saving her life."

"You are very welcome." Dr. Roberts returned to the OR.

Her doctor was right about everything so far. I just hope my chemo goes as smoothly as Mom's surgery did.

Right then, I called Dr. Selton and informed him of my intention to begin chemotherapy. He was relieved at my decision. Even though it scares the living crap out of me to go through with it, it's right thing to do. Not so much for me, but for my friends and loved ones. I can't just give up. I have to try and stay alive as long as I am able. I suspect that at the very last, it will be very difficult for me and everyone around me.

No matter what comes of that, I start chemo this coming Monday morning at 10:45. Let's hope the real healing begins.

The nurse came out and informed us, "Ms. Burrows is starting to wake up in the recovery room, and it shouldn't be too much longer before she will be returned to the third-floor ICU."

"Thank you. We will head that way now."

Mom passed us in the ICU waiting area on her way back to her room.

"Hello, children, it's nice to see you again. Ta ta."

I said, "Mom is feeling good, maybe a little too good. It must be the pain meds they gave her."

Vee piped in, "Yeah, that's got to be it."

We walked in on Mom grooming herself in her bathroom. The ICU nurse was assisting her as much as she would allow. As Mom got back into bed, I noticed she was having trouble manipulating her left hand.

I asked, "Mom, is your left hand, okay?"

"Yes, they said it may only be temporary. Physical therapy should help it recover. Don't worry, guys. Otherwise, I feel pretty good considering I have been asleep for a day and a half. I'm tired right now, I better try and get some rest before they come in and transfer what's left of my blood into a test tube."

Vee, Bea, and I looked worried to death. "Just relax, I'm going to be okay. Go home and get some rest. I am sure I will see you tomorrow."

Begrudgingly, we granted her request. I was exhausted anyway from sleeping on that pullout couch that was as comfortable as lying on a sheet of plywood. When Vee and I got home, I went straight to bed; I couldn't sleep. I kept thinking about Mom. She just had brain surgery, and she is more optimistic than I am.

Tomorrow is Friday. I start my chemotherapy in four days. I guess I should focus most of my energies on my Mom. Apparently, the stroke wasn't as bad as we thought. Hopefully, we will know more tomorrow. My treatments are going to go on for nine weeks. They gave me a whole list of really shitty side effects to expect. Everything from hair loss to projectile vomiting. I can't wait. I know this much for sure, if my cancer keeps spreading, no amount of treatment is going to do a damn bit of good. Screw this, I am going to take two aspirin and start over in the morning. Vee came in a few minutes. We lay together for a while, and I was able to relax.

I got up early the next three mornings, went surfing, and took walks with Vee. Mom is doing okay. They are starting to lower her pain meds so she can transfer to a surgical rehab facility. The docs said Tuesday or Wednesday is looking favorable. That is good news for her.

I managed to survive my first chemotherapy session. The medication/poison is given intravenously. Vee drove me there and back home. I ate a little bit, then lay down on the couch and fell asleep watching a college baseball game. I am not going to enjoy another eight weeks of this. The medication that I was prescribed helps with the nausea, but it is certainly not a cure-all. I still feel nauseous when I stand up.

Halfway through the treatments, they did a biopsy on my lymph nodes. It wasn't good. The cancer has spread pretty much everywhere. I don't know what is worse, knowing or not knowing. One thing is for sure: I am not going to my next birthday in ten months. It's too bad, because I love birthday cake and ice cream. My medical team gave me the standard five-to-six-month prognosis. They were just being kind. My appetite is less. I am losing weight. I would do anything for one of Mom's birthday cakes right now.

It seemed like almost every month, someone was having a birthday. The presents were always what we wanted, within reason, and the food as well. One year, Beatrice asked for a Venison roast. I don't know where they got it or what Mom did to prepare that roast, but it was amazing. I always picked lasagna. Mom was such a marvelous cook. Most of the local restaurants could not keep up with Martha's kitchen, as we used to affectionately call it. She made all the cakes too. Five-layer cakes filled with whatever we wanted inside. I loved her raspberry filling; the lemon was really good too. Dad would make homemade ice cream in whatever flavor we wanted. Mom and Dad made birthdays super special for us kids.

The nurse came into my room and told me I was done for the day, and the doctor would touch base with you in a day or so. I walked out to the lobby where Vee was sitting. I told her we could leave now.

"Will, how did the treatment go?"

"The same as the others. Thank goodness I'm over halfway done. I told you about the results of the biopsy. My memory ain't so good right now."

"Yes, you told me yesterday. Well, maybe the rest of the chemo will help you toward another remission."

"I hope so. Well, just have to wait and see." I thought to myself, I can guess what my next set of test results is going to be. They will be slightly worse than before. At this point, it's like chemotherapy is just giving me something to do on Mondays.

"Vee, can we stop by and visit Mom on the way home?"

"Sure, we haven't seen her in a couple of days. It looks like they are going to let her go home soon. It sounds like she is driving the kitchen staff nuts. I can't believe the food is that bad."

"I'm surprised Mom isn't supervising all the meals. She can't stand boring cuisine."

We found Mom in the recreation room playing cards with three other patients. They seemed to be having a good time, despite their situation. Mom looked really good. All her color was back in those rosy cheeks of hers.

"Hi Mom, how's it going?"

"Not good, son. Sheryl and I are getting waxed at canasta. Have a seat, this slaughter will be over shortly. They are up 3000 points on us." Vee and I walked over to the cafeteria and got coffee and a pastry. Mom showed up a few minutes later.

"It's good to see you getting around so well."

"I'm fine. I should be out of here next week. The question is, how are you doing with your chemo?"

"The treatment is not going very well. The cancer has spread elsewhere into my lymph nodes. The prognosis is months now instead of years."

"Sweetie, I'm so sorry. Are you in a great deal of pain right now?"

"No, right now it is mostly nausea and incontinence. The diapers actually work, believe it or not. I can't forget the shrinking appetite and weight loss. I have been dropping a couple of pounds a week. Soon, I will have to check into a hospice facility when the pain pills are no longer effective. Excuse me, I need to go to the bathroom."

Vee waited until I was out of hearing range. "Mom, Will is dying on me." She started to cry.

"Save your tears, honey, that beautiful man is going to need you and the entire family more than you know very soon. You have got to try and be strong for him. Talk to grief counselors if you have to. It helps to talk to someone else, even friends. It's going to get intense for you. Don't let yourself get all knotted up inside. Let it out, honey. Go talk to people who know how to help you through this. Losing a man that you dearly love is never easy. God knows how much I cried over Phillips' passing. I survived it because he wanted me to. Just like Will wants you to go on living so that you can find peace and joy again."

"Okay, I will do my best. I love you, Mom."

Will came back from the bathroom. He looked a little flushed, like he had been vomiting or suffering from diarrhea. Will and Vee said goodbye and headed home.

***

It is now very apparent to me that I am going to outlive at least one of my children. I never prepared myself for this type of scenario. I just assumed that all my precious babies would outlive me. I don't know who will be grieving the most, me or Veronica. I guess we will have to face Will's eventual passing together. I think I will offer to go with her to grief counseling. I am sure I will need an objective opinion at some point. If nothing else, to justify all the homemade motherly advice I have been doling out these past several weeks. It sounds good when I hear it, but I am not 100% sure it is the best medicine for everyone involved. One thing is for sure: Will is going to die of cancer, and there is nothing on this earth that will stop that tragedy from happening.

Chapter 22:
What Remains

As Vee drove us back to the house, I started getting really strong stomach cramps.

"Honey, I think you'd better take me to the emergency room. I have got horrible gas pain in my stomach. Oh crap, this really hurts!!"

"Hang on, Will, the hospital is about a mile away." Vee drove up to the ER, and I almost fell out of the passenger seat of the truck into a wheelchair. Vee wheeled me right up to the nurse and told them of my situation. An orderly ran out and took me back to one of the empty beds. I was still grimacing in pain. The nurse tried to ascertain where I was hurting. All I could tell her was that my gut was on fire! The doctor came in and I could barely hear him.

I woke up and had no idea where I was. A nurse was standing over me, trying to get my attention.

"Mr. Burrows, can you hear me? Are you awake, sir?"

"Yeah, I am awake. Where the hell am I?"

"You are in OR recovery. You just went through an appendectomy. You are very fortunate you got here when you did." The surgeon came in and introduced himself.

"Hello, Mr. Burrows, nice to see you again. I just removed your appendix. It was severely inflamed. How do you feel?"

"Well, doc, my gut isn't on fire anymore, thank you."

"Okay, we are going to keep you here overnight for observation. You should be released in the morning."

"I look forward to it. Thanks again for everything."

"You are very welcome." About half an hour later, the nurse wheeled me up to my room. At this point, all I wanted to do was go to the bathroom and sleep for a while. My life is not simple anymore. I don't really want to die right now, but it would appear this is the hand I have been dealt. If there is any truth to this whole karma thing, I hope I come back as an artist of some kind. I guess it has always been my hope that when I eventually died, I would somehow make everything around me a little more beautiful each day. I always tried to be the best version of myself. Maybe after my spirit has passed on, people will reflect and say Will Burrows was the most decent man I ever knew. I will be sorry to see him go. That is what I want, to be remembered as a kind, fortunate, decent man. My ending on this earth is not quite what I expected, but I think, under the circumstances, I can accept God's purpose for me in the time I was given. My light will forever dim so that others may shine bright instead.

The End

www.ingramcontent.com/pod-product-compliance
Lightning Source LLC
Chambersburg PA
CBHW051152120626
46547CB00012B/1052